PAUL V. DYNAMO SPORTING GOODS, DILLON, AND HANSON

A MOTION PRACTICE CASE STUDY

Third Edition
Materials for A's

D1710389

PAUL V. DYNAMO SPORTING GOODS, DILLON, AND HANSON

A MOTION PRACTICE CASE STUDY

Third Edition
Materials for A's

Morgan Cloud
Charles Howard Candler Professor of Law
Emory University

Mary Pat Dooley

Terre Rushton

Hon. Nancy Harris Vaidik
Chief Judge
Indiana Court of Appeals

NATIONAL INSTITUTE FOR TRIAL ADVOCACY

Address inquiries to:

Reprint Permission
National Institute for Trial Advocacy
1685 38th Street, Suite 200
Boulder, CO 80301-2735
Phone: (800) 225-6482
Fax: (720) 890-7069
Email: permissions@nita.org

ISBN 978-1-60156-749-9
eISBN 978-1-60156-7-505
FBA 1749

Printed in the United States of America

SUSTAINABLE FORESTRY INITIATIVE
Certified Sourcing
www.forests.org
SFI-01051

Official co-publisher of NITA.
WKLegaledu.com/NITA

CONTENTS

MATERIALS FOR A'S

Motions and Materials For Program

Acknowledgement

The authors would like to thank Facebook for permission to use a likeness of its web page in this case file.

IMPORTANT INFORMATION

1. This case file is completely fictitious and any resemblance to any person living or dead is coincidental and should not be misconstrued.

2. The dates in this case file are stated in the following form:

    o   YR-0 is this year

    o   YR-1 is last year (this year minus one year)

    o   YR-2 is two years ago (this year minus two years)

    o   YR-3 is three years ago (this year minus three years), and so on.

3. Upon filing the Answer, the Defendants filed for a TRO and a Preliminary Injunction. The TRO was denied, but expedited discovery was granted and the Preliminary Injunction in this matter was set.

4. All of the case law you will use in this program is provided to you. You should not do any additional legal research and no other sources are allowed. Note that almost every case has been redacted to provide you with only the part of the opinion that the authors believe is relevant to your arguments.

5. Possible arguments for each side are included in the case file. Although you should not do any independent legal research, you are not required to use these arguments nor are you limited to these arguments.

6. With the exception of Michelle Paul and Arthur Dillon, all witnesses are written to be gender and race neutral. They may be played by a person of any gender or ethnic background.

7. Copies of the exhibits are available online at:

http://bit.ly/1P20Jea
Password: Paul3

PLEADINGS

IN THE UNITED STATES DISTRICT COURT
FOR THE DISTRICT OF NITA

MICHELLE PAUL, Plaintiff	)))	
v.	)))	CIVIL ACTION NO. YR-1-1234
DYNAMO SPORTING GOODS, a corporation,	)))	JURY TRIAL DEMANDED
ARTHUR DILLON,	))	
and	))	
SAM HANSON, Defendants	))	

COMPLAINT

PARTIES

1. Plaintiff, Michelle Paul (Paul), is an adult individual, who is a citizen of Georgia and of the United States. She resides in Atlanta, Georgia.

2. Defendant, Dynamo Sporting Goods (Dynamo), is a corporation incorporated under the laws of the State of Nita, with its offices and principal place of business located at Four Independence Industrial Park, Nita City, Nita.

3(a). Defendant, Arthur Dillon (Dillon), is an adult individual who is a citizen of New York and the United States. He resides in New York City, New York.

3(b). Defendant Dillon, at all times material to this lawsuit, was and continues to be, president and sole shareholder of Dynamo Sporting Goods.

4. Defendant, Sam Hanson (Hanson), is an adult individual who is a citizen of Connecticut and the United States. He resides in Old Greenwich, Connecticut.

JURISDICTION AND VENUE

5. Jurisdiction is founded on diversity of citizenship and amount. Plaintiff invokes this court's jurisdiction pursuant to 28 U.S.C. § 1332. Plaintiff is a citizen of the State of Georgia. Defendant Arthur Dillon is a citizen of the State of New York, and Defendant Dynamo Sporting Goods is a corporation incorporated under the laws of the State of Nita, having its principal place of business in a State other

than Georgia. The matter in controversy exceeds, exclusive of interest and costs, the sum of $1 million dollars.

6. Venue is appropriate in the District of Nita because one of the Defendants resides in the State of Nita, the claims arose there, and the Defendants may all be served with process.

CLAIM I

(Breach of Contract)

7. Plaintiff incorporates and reasserts by reference the allegations set forth in Paragraphs 1 through 6 as if set forth fully herein.

8. On or about March 24, YR-3, at Paul's offices in Georgia, Plaintiff and Defendant Dillon executed a Memorandum of Agreement, in which Defendant Dillon agreed to purchase Sportslifeware, a business owned and operated by Plaintiff as a sole proprietorship. A copy of the Memorandum of Agreement is attached hereto and incorporated herein by reference as if set forth herein in full.

9. According to the terms of the Memorandum of Agreement, Defendant Dillon agreed to purchase Sportslifeware for a total purchase price of $6 million, plus interest. Defendant Dillon agreed to make a cash payment of $500,000 at the closing of the transaction, and to pay to Plaintiff the remaining portion of the purchase price, $5.5 million, together with interest, not later than September 1, YR-2.

10. To persuade Plaintiff to accept the deferred payment of $5.5 million plus interest, Defendant Dillon agreed to personally guarantee the payment of the purchase price. To persuade Plaintiff to accept his personal guarantee, on or about March 24, YR-3, Defendant Dillon supplied Plaintiff with a personal financial statement that purported to demonstrate that Defendant Dillon had a net financial worth of $13 million. A copy of Dillon's Personal Financial Statement dated March 23, YR-3, is attached hereto and incorporated herein by reference as if set forth herein in full.

11. In the Memorandum of Agreement, Defendant Dillon also agreed that at the time of the closing of the purchase and sale of Sportslifeware, he would provide Plaintiff with a financial statement current and accurate at the time of the closing. Seller agreed to complete the purchase and sale transaction only if Defendant Dillon's net financial worth at the time of closing was not less than $13 million.

12. On or about December 30, YR-3, at Dynamo's and Dillon's offices in Nita City, Plaintiff and Defendants Dynamo and Dillon executed an Asset Purchase Agreement by which Plaintiff sold and Defendants Dynamo and Dillon purchased all assets of the Company Sportslifeware. Defendant Hanson drafted the Asset Purchase Agreement. A copy of the Asset Purchase Agreement is attached hereto and incorporated herein by reference as if set forth herein in full.

13. Pursuant to the terms of the Asset Purchase Agreement, Defendants Dynamo and Dillon agreed to pay a total purchase price of $6 million, plus interest. Pursuant to the terms of the Agreement, these Defendants made a cash payment of $500,000 at the closing of the transaction, and promised to pay

to Plaintiff the additional sum of $5.5 million, plus interest calculated at the rate of 8 percent per year, not later than September 1, YR-2.

14. To induce Plaintiff to enter into the transaction, Defendants Dynamo, Dillon, and Hanson provided Plaintiff with a Personal Guaranty of Payment and Performance (Personal Guaranty), executed by Dillon on December 30, YR-3, together with a Personal Financial Statement dated December 23, YR-3, purporting to demonstrate that Defendant Dillon had a net financial worth exceeding $13 million. The Personal Financial Statement dated December 23, YR-3, was contained in a group of closing documents delivered to Plaintiff by Defendant Hanson. A copy of the Personal Guaranty and a copy of Dillon's Personal Financial Statement dated December 23, YR-3, are attached hereto and incorporated herein by reference as if set forth herein in full.

15. Plaintiff has performed all of her obligations under the terms of the Memorandum of Agreement dated March 24, YR-3.

16. Plaintiff has performed all of her obligations under the terms of the Asset Purchase Agreement dated December 30, YR-3.

17. Defendants Dynamo and Dillon breached their obligations under the Memorandum of Agreement and the Asset Purchase Agreement by failing to pay the sum of $5.5 million, plus interest, due on or before September 1, YR-2. Despite repeated demands by Plaintiff, Defendants continue to refuse to pay the sums due under terms of these Agreements.

18. As a result of Defendants' breach of their contractual obligations, Plaintiff has suffered damages in excess of $6 million.

CLAIM II

(Fraud in the Inducement)

19. Plaintiff incorporates and reasserts by reference paragraphs 1 through 18 as if set forth fully herein.

20. Based upon information and belief, between March 23, YR-3, and December 23, YR-3, Defendants Dynamo and Dillon suffered financial setbacks. On December 23, YR-3, and at the time of the closing, Defendant Dillon had a personal net financial worth of less than $13 million. Although each of the Defendants possessed personal knowledge of these facts, they failed to disclose these facts to Plaintiff.

21. On information and belief, Plaintiff alleges that defendants Dillon and Dynamo had direct and personal knowledge of their own financial condition and that Defendant Hanson had direct and personal knowledge of Defendants Dillon and Dynamo's financial condition as a result of his representation of the Defendants in this and other legal and financial dealings. Dillon admitted to Plaintiff and Hanson reaffirmed to the Plaintiff's attorney that he was intimately aware of Dillon and Dynamo's finances.

22. In July YR-3, Defendant Hanson and the attorney for the Plaintiff talked about Plaintiff's concern that Defendants Dillon and Dynamo would not be able to purchase Sportslifeware. Plaintiff's attorney told Defendant Hanson that Plaintiff had second thoughts about the sale and was willing to walk away from the Memorandum of Agreement. Defendant Hanson replied that Defendants Dillon and Dynamo would meet the terms of the agreement, and that he would personally review and handle all closing documents and financial matters to make sure that they were fine.

23. On or about December 23, YR-3, defendant Dillon executed a Personal Financial Statement indicating he had a personal net worth exceeding $13 million, knowing the statements were false, and made them intentionally for the purpose of inducing the Plaintiff to sell her business, Sportslifeware.

24. On or about December 29, YR-3, Defendant Hanson delivered the Personal Financial Statement to Plaintiff through her attorney, knowing the statements were false, holding himself out as knowledgeable of Dillon's finances, representing in an email to Plaintiff's counsel that he had reviewed all closing documents including the Personal Financial Statement and that they were fine, while failing to disclose his knowledge that the Personal Financial Statement was not accurate and that Dillon's personal net worth was under $13 million, when he had a duty to disclose the information, all done for the purpose of inducing the Plaintiff to sell her business.

25. Plaintiff expressly relied upon Defendants' intentional false and fraudulent statements. As a result, she was induced to enter into the Asset Purchase Agreement, by which Defendants defrauded Plaintiff of her business and all of its assets, causing Plaintiff to suffer actual damages in excess of $6 million.

WHEREFORE, Plaintiff prays that this Court will:

A. Enter judgment in favor of Plaintiff and against Defendants Arthur Dillon and Dynamo Sporting Goods for compensatory damages resulting from Defendants' breach of contract, in an amount exceeding $6 million, together with interest.

B. Enter judgment in favor of Plaintiff and against Defendants Arthur Dillon, Dynamo Sporting Goods, and Sam Hanson for compensatory damages resulting from Defendants' fraud in inducing Plaintiff to enter into the contract in an amount exceeding $6 million, together with interest.

C. Enter judgment in favor of Plaintiff, and against Defendants Arthur Dillon, Dynamo Sporting Goods, and Sam Hanson for compensatory damages, including, but not limited to, damages for mental anguish and humiliation, together with interest, resulting from Defendants' fraudulent conduct.

D. Enter judgment in favor of Plaintiff, and against Defendants Arthur Dillon, Dynamo Sporting Goods, and Sam Hanson for punitive damages, including, but not limited to, damages for mental anguish and humiliation, together with interest, resulting from Defendants' intentional tortious conduct.

E. Award Plaintiff reasonable attorneys' fees together with the costs of this action.

F. Award such other and further legal and equitable relief as may be appropriate to redress Plaintiff fully for the harm suffered as a result of the Defendants' conduct

JURY DEMAND

Plaintiff demands a jury trial for all claims triable by a jury.

Respectfully submitted,

Donald Davis, Esquire
1500 Main Street
Nita City, Nita 00176

Dated: March 2, YR-1

VERIFICATION

I, Michelle Paul, am the Plaintiff in the above-captioned action.

I have read this complaint and verify that the allegations in it are true.

Michelle Paul

Signed and sworn before me this 2nd day of March, YR-1.

Notary Public

ATTACHMENTS: (1) MEMORANDUM OF AGREEMENT, (2) PERSONAL FINANCIAL STATEMENT DATED MARCH 23, YR-3, (3) PERSONAL FINANCIAL STATEMENT DATED DECEMBER 23, YR-3, (4) PERSONAL GUARANTY ARE ATTACHED TO THE COMPLAINT*

*These documents will be found beginning at page 21 of this book.

IN THE UNITED STATES DISTRICT COURT
FOR THE DISTRICT OF NITA

MICHELLE PAUL, Plaintiff	)	
	)	
	)	
v.	)	
	)	CIVIL ACTION NO.
ARTHUR DILLON,	)	YR-1-1234
	)	
and	)	
	)	JURY TRIAL DEMANDED
DYNAMO SPORTING GOODS, a corporation,	)	
	)	
and	)	
	)	
SAM HANSON, Defendants	)	

**ANSWER AND AFFIRMATIVE DEFENSES OF DEFENDANTS
DYNAMO SPORTING GOODS, a corporation, ARTHUR DILLON,
and SAM HANSON**

By way of answer, Defendants Arthur Dillon, Dynamo Sporting Goods, and Sam Hanson respond to Plaintiff's allegations as follows:

1. Admit.

2. Admit.

3(a). Admit.

3(b). Admit.

4. Admit.

5. Admit, except that Defendants deny that jurisdiction is proper in the United States District Court for the District of Nita.

6. Deny.

7. Deny all allegations incorporated by reference that were heretofore denied, and admit those allegations incorporated by reference that were already admitted.

8. Admit.

9. Admit.

10. Admit that Defendant Dillon provided a personal financial statement to Plaintiff, but deny all other allegations in Paragraph 10.

11. Admit that Defendant Dillon agreed to provide a personal financial statement to Plaintiff, but deny all other allegations in Paragraph 11.

12. Admit that Defendant Hanson drafted the Agreement based upon terms agreed to by the Plaintiff and Defendant Dillon, and admit all other allegations contained in Paragraph 12.

13. Admit.

14. Defendants admit that Defendant Dillon provided Plaintiff with a personal financial statement included with the closing documents, but deny all other allegations in Paragraph 14.

15. Deny.

16. Deny.

17. Deny.

18. Deny.

19. Deny all allegations incorporated by reference that were heretofore denied, and admit those allegations incorporated by reference that were already admitted.

20. Deny, except Defendants are unable to admit or deny any allegations concerning the Defendants' "financial condition" because these allegations are too vague and ambiguous to be answered.

21. Deny.

22. Deny.

23. Deny.

24. Deny.

25. Deny.

FIRST AFFIRMATIVE DEFENSE

Defendants aver for an affirmative defense that Plaintiff has failed to state a claim upon which relief can be granted.

SECOND AFFIRMATIVE DEFENSE

Defendants aver for an affirmative defense that Plaintiff was guilty of unfair trade practices by obtaining and using trade secrets and confidential information in violation of the Agreements between Plaintiff and Defendants Dynamo Sporting Goods and Dillon, and therefore Plaintiff is barred by the doctrine of unclean hands.

THIRD AFFIRMATIVE DEFENSE

Defendants aver for an affirmative defense that Plaintiff is estopped from asserting the provisions of the Asset Purchase Agreement due to Plaintiff's own conduct that violates the provisions of that Agreement.

COUNTERCLAIM OF DYNAMO SPORTING GOODS AND ARTHUR DILLON
FIRST CLAIM FOR RELIEF
(Breach of Contract)

Defendants Dynamo Sporting Goods, a corporation (Dynamo), and Arthur Dillon (Dillon), by way of a Counterclaim against the Plaintiff Michelle Paul (Paul), aver as follows:

1. On or about December 30, YR-3, at Dynamo and Dillon's offices in Nita City, Dynamo, Dillon, and Paul executed an Asset Purchase Agreement (Agreement) in which Dynamo and Dillon agreed to purchase Sportslifeware, a business owned and operated by Plaintiff as a sole proprietorship. A copy of the Asset Purchase Agreement is attached hereto and incorporated herein by reference as if set forth herein in full.

2. According to the terms of the Asset Purchase Agreement, Dynamo and Dillon agreed to purchase Sportslifeware for a total purchase price of $6 million, plus interest. Dynamo and Dillon agreed to make a cash payment of $500,000 at the closing of the transaction, which payment was made in full, and to pay to Plaintiff the remaining portion of the purchase price, $5.5 million, together with interest, not later than September 1, YR-2.

3. To persuade and induce Dynamo and Dillon to enter into this Agreement, Paul agreed to Covenants of Non-Competition and Confidentiality of Trade Secrets (Covenants), contained in Paragraph 5.04 and elsewhere in the Agreement. Pursuant to the terms of the Agreement, Paul agreed to sell to Dynamo and Dillon "all right, title and interest in certain trade secrets and confidential information used in the Business" of Sportslifeware (the Business).

4. In the Agreement, Paul specifically agreed and promised not to obtain or use confidential information and trade secrets of the Business in any other business, operations, or activities.

5. Paul breached the terms of the Agreement by obtaining and using confidential information and trade secrets of the Business in her other business, operations, and activities.

6. In the Agreement, Paul also covenanted that for a period of three years from and after the date of the Agreement, she would use reasonable efforts to ensure that her representatives or affiliates will not solicit customers and employees of the Business.

7. Paul breached her obligations under the Agreement by acting, within a period of three years from and after the date of the Agreement, to solicit customers and employees of the Business, either directly, or by and through her representatives or affiliates, or both.

8. As a result of Defendant's breach of her contractual obligations, Dynamo and Dillon have suffered damages in excess of $2 million.

CLAIM II

(Fraud in the Inducement)

9. Dynamo and Dillon incorporate and reassert by reference paragraphs 1 through 8 as if set forth fully herein.

10. Despite the terms of the Covenants executed by Paul on December 30, YR-3, at all times relevant to this action, including times before and at or about the time of the Agreement, Paul intended to solicit customers and employees of the Business, all in violation of the terms of the Covenant and the Agreement. Paul executed the Covenants despite her intent to violate the Agreement's express terms, for the purpose of fraudulently inducing Dynamo and Dillon to enter into the Agreement. At all relevant times, Paul knew the promises contained in the Covenants were false and made them intentionally for the purpose of inducing Dynamo and Dillon to enter into the Agreement to purchase the Business.

11. Dynamo and Dillon expressly relied upon Paul's intentional false and fraudulent statements, which induced them to enter into the Agreement, causing Dynamo and Dillon to suffer actual damages in excess of $2 million.

CLAIM III

(Unfair Competition)

12. Dynamo and Dillon incorporate and reassert by reference paragraphs 1 through 11 as if set forth fully herein.

13. After the sale of Sportslifeware to Dynamo and Dillon, Paul started a business, "Sportique," which manufactures and sells sportswear in competition with Dynamo and Dillon.

14. Paul has unfairly competed with Dynamo and Dillon by undertaking a deliberate plan of soliciting and hiring key employees of Dynamo and Dillon, by inducing these key employees to misappropriate trade secrets and confidential information owned by Dynamo and Dillon, by misappropriation of trade secrets and confidential information owned by Dynamo and Dillon, and by soliciting customers of Dynamo and Dillon, all in violation of the terms of the Asset Purchase Agreement. As a result of these acts, Paul has obtained an immediate marketability and salability of her products, in direct competition with Dynamo and Dillon and their products, which she would not have obtained without her misappropriation and exploitation of Dynamo and Dillon's trade secrets and confidential information and her wrongful solicitation and hiring of Dynamo and Dillon's key employees. Paul's

actions constitute unfair competition, which has caused Dynamo and Dillon to suffer great, substantial, and irreparable damage.

WHEREFORE, Counter-Plaintiffs pray that this Court will:

A. Enter judgment in favor of Arthur Dillon and Dynamo for compensatory damages resulting from Paul's breach of contract, in an amount exceeding $3 million, together with interest.

B. Enter judgment in favor of Arthur Dillon and Dynamo and against Paul for compensatory damages resulting from Paul's fraud in inducing Counter-Plaintiffs to enter into the contract in an amount exceeding $3 million, together with interest.

C. Enter judgment in favor of Arthur Dillon and for compensatory damages, including but not limited to, damages for mental anguish and humiliation, together with interest, resulting from Paul's fraudulent conduct.

D. Enter judgment in favor of Arthur Dillon and Dynamo for punitive damages, including but not limited to, damages for mental anguish and humiliation, together with interest, resulting from Paul's intentional tortious conduct.

E. Temporarily and permanently enjoin and restrain Paul, her agents, employees, and all others from:

1. further use and/or disclosure of Dynamo and Arthur Dillon's trade secrets and confidential information.

2. doing any act in breach of the Covenants not to solicit Dynamo and Arthur Dillon's customers.

3. doing any act in breach of the Covenants not to solicit or hire employees of Dynamo and Arthur Dillon, including but not limited to, those having any knowledge of or access to Dynamo and Arthur Dillon's trade secrets and confidential information.

4. doing any other act calculated to, tending to, or likely to unfairly compete with Dynamo and Arthur Dillon.

F. Order Paul, her agents, employees, and all others to deliver up for destruction all materials, or any part thereof, embodying Dynamo and Arthur Dillon's trade secrets or confidential information.

G. Award Arthur Dillon and Dynamo reasonable attorneys' fees together with the costs of this action.

H. Award such other and further legal and equitable relief as may be appropriate to redress Dynamo and Arthur Dillon fully for the harm suffered as a result of Paul's conduct.

JURY DEMAND

Plaintiff demands a jury trial for all claims triable by a jury.

Respectfully submitted for the Counter-Plaintiffs,
Arthur Dillon, Dynamo Sporting Goods, and Sam Hanson

(Timely Filed, YR-1.)

Janet Meltzman

Janet Meltzman, Esq.
8800 Independence Way
Nita City, Nita 00911

VERIFICATION

I, Arthur Dillon, am the Counter-Plaintiff in the above-captioned action. I have read this Counterclaim and verify that the allegations in it are true.

Arthur Dillon

Arthur Dillon

Signed and sworn before me this date, YR-1.

Ashley Smith

Notary Public

IN THE UNITED STATES DISTRICT COURT
FOR THE DISTRICT OF NITA

MICHELLE PAUL,	)	
Plaintiff	)	
	)	
v.	)	CIVIL ACTION NO. YR-1-1234
	)	
ARTHUR DILLON, et al.	)	
Defendants	)	

PLAINTIFF AND COUNTER-DEFENDANT MICHELLE PAUL'S
ANSWER AND AFFIRMATIVE DEFENSES TO COUNTERCLAIMS

By way of answer, Plaintiff and Counter-Defendant, Michelle Paul (Paul), responds to Defendant's allegations in their Counterclaims as follows:

1. Admit.

2. Admit.

3. Deny that Plaintiff and Counter-Defendant acted to induce Defendants to enter into the agreement, but otherwise admits the allegations contained in Paragraph 3.

4. Deny.

5. Deny.

6. Admit.

7. Deny.

8. Deny.

9. Deny all allegations incorporated by reference that were heretofore denied, and admit those allegations incorporated by reference that were already admitted.

10. Deny.

11. Deny.

12. Deny all allegations incorporated by reference that were heretofore denied, and admit those allegations incorporated by reference that were already admitted.

13. Admits that she has started a business operating under the name Sportique, but otherwise denies the allegations contained in paragraph 13.

14. Deny.

FIRST AFFIRMATIVE DEFENSE

Paul avers for an affirmative defense that Counter-Plaintiff have failed to state a claim upon which relief can be granted.

SECOND AFFIRMATIVE DEFENSE

Paul avers for an affirmative defense that Counter-Plaintiffs and Defendants Dynamo Sporting Goods and Dillon are guilty of committing intentional fraud against Paul, and therefore are barred by the doctrine of unclean hands.

THIRD AFFIRMATIVE DEFENSE

Paul avers for an affirmative defense that Counter-Plaintiffs are estopped from asserting the provisions of the Asset Purchase Agreement due to their own intentional conduct that violates the provisions of that Agreement.

Respectfully submitted,

Donald Davis, Esquire
1500 Main Street
Nita City, Nita 00176

(Timely Filed, YR-1.)

VERIFICATION

I, Michelle Paul, am the Counter-Defendant in the above-captioned action. I have read this pleading and verify that the allegations in it are true.

Michelle Paul

Michelle Paul

Signed and sworn before me this date, YR-1.

Ashley Smith

Notary Public

TRANSACTION DOCUMENTS

Memorandum of Agreement

This Memorandum of Agreement, dated March 24, YR-3, is intended to reflect the intentions of Michelle Paul, "Seller," and Arthur Dillon and Dynamo Sporting Goods, "Buyer," to carry out the following transaction.

1. Seller is sole owner and sole proprietor of Sportslifeware, a manufacturer of sportswear and other apparel. Buyer is sole shareholder and president of Dynamo Sporting Goods, which manufactures and distributes athletic equipment.

2. Seller agrees to sell all of her right, title, and interest in Sportslifeware to Buyer for a total price of $6 million.

3. Buyer agrees to pay the total purchase price of $6 million, according to the following payment schedule: (a) $500,000 to be paid at closing, which will be held on a date selected by Buyer, but not later than December 31, YR-3. (b) The remaining balance of the purchase price, $5.5 million, together with interest, shall be due on or before September 1, YR-2. Interest shall be calculated at a rate to be decided upon by the parties prior to the closing.

4. To facilitate this transaction, Buyer agrees to execute a personal guarantee of the payment of the purchase price. To demonstrate his ability to fulfill such a guarantee, Buyer has provided Seller with a current and accurate financial statement, a copy of which is attached to this Memorandum of Agreement. Buyer further agrees to provide an updated financial statement to Seller at the closing, which is current and accurate at that time. Buyer and Seller agree that Seller will be free to terminate this agreement if the Buyer's financial statement at the time of closing demonstrates that Buyer's net worth is less than $13 million.

5. The documents necessary for the closing will be prepared by Buyer's attorneys at Buyer's expense.

Signed this 24th day of March, YR-3.

Michelle Paul
_____
Michelle Paul, Seller

Arthur Dillon
_____
Arthur Dillon, Buyer

ASSET PURCHASE AGREEMENT*

BACKGROUND

This ASSET PURCHASE AGREEMENT is made this 30th day of December, YR-3, by and among Michelle Paul (Seller), Arthur Dillon, and Dynamo Sporting Goods, a corporation (Purchaser).

BACKGROUND

Seller is engaged in the business of designing and manufacturing sportswear, as the sole proprietor of Sportslifeware (the business). Seller is the owner of, and desires to sell, and Purchaser desires to purchase substantially all of the assets of Seller related to the business upon the terms and subject to the conditions set forth herein. Therefore, the parties agree to the following:

ARTICLE I
PURCHASE AND SALE OF ASSETS

1.01 Purchase of the Assets. Subject to the terms and conditions of this agreement, at the closing, Seller shall sell, convey, transfer, assign, and deliver to Purchaser and Purchaser shall purchase and accept from Seller all of the assets, free and clear of any and all liens.

1.02 Purchase Price. The total purchase price for the acquisition of the assets shall be $6 million.

1.03 Payment of Cash Portion of the Purchase Price. On the closing date, Purchaser shall pay the cash portion of the purchase price to Seller by delivering to the Seller the sum of $500,000, by wire transfer of immediately available funds, or in such other form and manner as may be mutually satisfactory.

1.04 Payment of Remainder of the Purchase Price. On or before September 1, YR-2, Buyer shall pay to Seller the sum of $5.5 million, by wire transfer of immediately available funds, or in such other form and manner as may be mutually satisfactory, together with interest calculated from the date of the closing until the date of payment at the rate of 8 percent per year.

1.05 Closing. The closing shall take place at the offices of Dynamo Sporting Goods, Four Independence Industrial Park, Nita City, Nita 00911, on the closing date. Title to the assets shall pass from Seller to Purchaser upon the closing unless the parties shall otherwise have agreed in writing.

ARTICLE II
ASSUMPTIONOF LIABILITIES

2.01 General. Nothing contained in this Section 2.01 or in any instrument of assumption executed by Purchaser at the closing shall be deemed to release or relieve Seller from any respective representations, warranties, covenants, and agreements contained in this agreement or any of the other agreements,

---

* For your convenience, only the titles and the pertinent sections of the lengthy contract are reproduced herein.

including, without limitation, the obligations of Seller to indemnify Purchaser in accordance with the provisions of Article VIII.

* * *

ARTICLE III
REPRESENTATIONS AND WARRANTIES OF SELLER

* * *

ARTICLE IV
REPRESENTATIONS AND WARRANTIES OF PURCHASER

Purchaser hereby represents and warrants to Seller that:

* * *

4.02 Authority and Binding Effect. Purchaser has the corporate power and authority necessary to enter into and perform its obligations under this agreement and the other agreements and to consummate the transactions contemplated hereby and thereby. The execution, delivery, and performance of this agreement and the other agreements have been or will as of the closing date be approved by all necessary action of the directors and shareholders of Purchaser. This agreement has been, and the other agreements will be, executed and delivered by duly authorized officers of Purchaser and each constitutes, or will constitute when executed and delivered, the legal, valid, and binding obligation of Purchaser, enforceable against Purchaser in accordance with its terms.

4.03 Statements True and Correct. No representation or warranty made by Purchaser, nor any statement, certificate, or instrument furnished or to be furnished to Seller pursuant to this agreement or any other document, agreement, or instrument referred to herein or therein, contains or will contain any untrue statement of material fact or omits or will omit to state a material fact necessary to make the statements contained therein not misleading.

ARTICLE V
COVENANTS AND ADDITIONAL AGREEMENTS
OF SELLER AND PURCHASER

5.01 Operation of Business Pending Closing. Prior to the closing date, except with the prior written consent of Purchaser and except as necessary to effect the transactions contemplated in this agreement, Seller shall:

(a) conduct its business in substantially the same manner as presently being conducted, and refrain from entering into any transaction or contract other than in the ordinary course of business consistent with past practice;

* * *

5.02 Confidentiality. For a period of three years from and after the date hereof, Purchaser and Seller, and both of them, agree not to use:

(a) any confidential or nonpublic information relating to the other parties to this agreement; or

(b) the existence of this agreement or the fact of the transactions contemplated hereby, except

(i) for a disclosure that is required by law or by a governmental authority or is reasonably believed to be so required, including, without limitation, disclosures to lottery commissions or authorities for purposes of obtaining consents to the transactions contemplated hereby;

(ii) information that is ascertainable or obtained from public or published information;

(iii) information received from a third party not known to the disclosing party to be under an obligation to keep such information confidential;

(iv) information independently developed by the disclosing party; or

(v) information disclosed to or filed with any persons necessary to obtaining the consents, the equity, and the financing relating to the transactions contemplated by this agreement.

5.03 Supplying Financial Statements of Seller. On or prior to the closing date, Seller shall deliver to Purchaser true and complete copies of unaudited balance sheets of Seller as of the closing date and the related statements of income and cash flows for the business. All such unaudited interim financial statements shall be in the same format as the financial statements.

5.04 Seller's Covenants of Confidentiality of Trade Secrets and Non-Competition Pursuant to this agreement, Seller agrees to sell to Purchaser all right, title, and interest in certain trade secrets and confidential information used in the business.

(a) <u>Definition of Trade Secrets.</u> For purposes of this agreement, a trade secret is any formula, pattern, device, method, technique, process, or compilation of information used in the business that provides the business with an opportunity to obtain an advantage over competitors who do not know or use it. Trade secrets include formulas, marketing plans, special manufacturing processes, sources of materials, product specifications, testing techniques, specialized customer lists, pricing information, and the expiration dates of customer contracts.

(b) <u>Covenants of Confidentiality.</u> Seller agrees that she will not, and will use reasonable efforts to ensure that her representatives, employees, successors in interest, and any purchaser of assets from Seller will not:

(i) disclose confidential information and trade secrets of the business as defined in this agreement; and

(ii) obtain or use confidential information and trade secrets of the business in any other business, operations, or activities.

(c) <u>Covenants of Non-Competition.</u> Seller also agrees that for a period of three years from and after the date hereof, Seller will not solicit employees of the business and will use reasonable efforts to ensure that her representatives, employees, successors in interest, and any purchaser of assets from Seller will not solicit employees of the business.

(d) <u>Other Covenants.</u> Seller shall cause each of her respective representatives, employees, and any successor in interest to, or purchaser of assets from, Seller to agree to the terms of the covenants and agreements set forth in this Agreement.

ARTICLE VI
CONDITIONS PRECEDENT TO OBLIGATIONS OF PURCHASER

The obligations of Purchaser to consummate the transactions contemplated by this agreement shall be subject to the satisfaction, on or before the closing date, of each of the following conditions, any of which may be waived, in whole or in part, by Purchaser for purposes of consummating such transactions, but without prejudice to any other right or remedy which Purchaser may have hereunder as a result of any misrepresentation by, or breach of any agreement, covenant or warranty of, Seller contained in this agreement or the other agreements:

6.01 Representations True and Covenants Performed at Closing. The representations and warranties made by Seller in this agreement and the other agreements shall be complete and correct on the closing date with the same force and effect as if this agreement had been executed on and as of the closing date. Seller shall have duly performed all of the agreements and covenants and satisfied all of the conditions to be performed or complied with by either of them on or prior to the closing date. Seller shall execute and deliver to Purchaser a certificate dated as of the closing date certifying the fulfillment of the conditions of this Section 6.01.

6.02 Appraisal. On or before the closing date, Purchaser shall have requested and received an independent appraisal of the assets of the business . . . .

6.03 Covenants Not To Compete. Seller shall have entered into agreements with Purchaser containing covenants not to compete and covenants prohibiting disclosure of confidential information and trade secrets and covenants prohibiting the solicitation of customers and employees. Further, Seller shall cause each of her respective affiliates and any person who is a successor in interest to, or a purchaser of assets from, Seller or any of her respective affiliates, to agree to the terms of such agreements.

ARTICLE VII
CONDITIONS PRECEDENT TO OBLIGATIONS OF SELLER

The obligations of Seller to consummate the transactions contemplated by this agreement shall be subject to the satisfaction, on or before the closing date, of each of the following conditions, any of which may be waived, in whole or in part, by Seller for purposes of consummating such transactions, but without prejudice to any other right or remedy which Seller may have hereunder as a result of any misrepresentation by, or breach of any agreement, covenant, or warranty of Purchaser contained in this agreement or the other agreements:

7.01 Representations True and Covenants Performed at Closing. The representations and warranties made by Purchaser in this agreement and the other agreements shall be correct and complete on the closing date with the same force and effect as if such this agreement had been executed on and as of the closing date. Purchaser shall have duly performed all of the agreements and covenants and satisfied all of the conditions to be performed or complied with by it on or prior to the closing date.

ARTICLE VIII
SURVIVAL OF REPRESENTATIONS AND WARRANTIES AND INDEMNIFICATION

8.01 Obligation of Seller to Indemnify. Subject to the limitations contained in this Section, Seller agrees to indemnify Purchaser and its officers, directors, employees, counsel, agents, and affiliates, and assigns against, and hold each of them harmless from, all losses asserted against, imposed upon, or incurred by any of the foregoing by reason of, resulting from, arising out of, based upon, or otherwise in respect of the following notwithstanding any actual or alleged negligence of any of the persons indemnified hereunder:

(a) any inaccuracy in any representation or warranty made by Seller pursuant to this agreement or the other agreements;

(b) any breach of any covenant or agreement made or to be performed by Seller pursuant to this agreement or the other agreements.

8.02 Obligation of Purchaser to Indemnify. Subject to the limitations contained in this section, Purchaser agrees to indemnify Seller and each of her respective officers, directors, employees, counsel, agents, and affiliates, and assigns against, and hold her harmless from, all losses asserted against, imposed upon, or incurred by any of the foregoing by reason of, resulting from, arising out of, based upon, or otherwise in respect of:

(a) any inaccuracy in any representation or warranty made by Purchaser pursuant to this agreement or the other agreements;

(b) any breach of any covenant or agreement made or to be performed by Purchaser pursuant to this agreement or the other agreements.

ARTICLE IX
TERMINATION

9.01 Method of Termination. This agreement and the transactions contemplated by it may be terminated at any time prior to the closing date:

(a) By the mutual consent of Seller and Purchaser at any time;

(b) By Seller at any time after closing date if any of the conditions set forth in Article VII hereof have not been fulfilled or waived, unless such fulfillment has been frustrated or made impossible by any act or failure to act by Seller;

(c) By Purchaser at any time after closing date, if any of the conditions set forth in Article VI hereof have not been fulfilled or waived, unless such fulfillment has been frustrated or made impossible by any act or failure to act by Purchaser.

IN WITNESS WHEREOF, the parties have caused their duly authorized representatives to execute this Agreement as of the date first above written.

SELLER:

By: *Michelle Paul*

Title: Owner, Sportslifeware

[CORPORATE SEAL]

PURCHASER:

By: *Arthur Dillon*

Title: President, Dynamo Sporting Goods

Personal Guaranty of Payment and Performance

ARTHUR DILLON ("Guarantor") hereby makes this PERSONAL GUARANTY this 30th day of December, YR-3, to induce Michelle Paul (Seller) to sell a business, Sportslifeware to Dynamo Sporting Goods, a corporation (Purchaser), according to the terms of the Asset Purchase Agreement executed by Seller, Purchaser, and Guarantor on this date. In consideration of the mutual covenants, agreements, representations, and warranties contained in the Asset Purchase Agreement entered into by Seller and Purchaser on this date, and agree as follows:

Seller is engaged in the business of designing and manufacturing sportswear, as the sole proprietor of Sportslifeware (the business). Seller is the owner of, and desires to sell, and Purchaser desires to purchase substantially all of the assets of Seller related to the business upon the terms and subject to the conditions set forth in the Asset Purchase Agreement entered into on this date.

Pursuant to the terms of the Asset Purchase Agreement entered into this date by Seller and Purchaser, Purchaser agrees to pay a total purchase price for the acquisition of the Assets that shall be equal to (i) the amount of the assumed liabilities plus (ii) $6 million. According to the terms of the Asset Purchase Agreement, on the Closing Date, Purchaser shall pay a portion of the Purchase Price to Seller by delivering to the Seller the sum of $500,000, by wire transfer of immediately available funds, or in such other form and manner as may be mutually satisfactory. On or before September 1, YR-2, Buyer shall pay to Seller the sum of $5.5 million, by wire transfer of immediately available funds, or in such other form and manner as may be mutually satisfactory, together with interest calculated from the date of the closing until the date of payment at the rate of 8 percent per year.

Guarantor does hereby unconditionally guarantee to Seller and her successors and assigns the full and prompt payment when due, with such interest as may accrue thereon, either before or after maturity thereof, all sums due to Seller pursuant to the terms of the Asset Purchase Agreement, and to pay said sums should Purchaser default in its obligations. Guarantor does hereby agree that if Purchaser fails to make full and prompt payment to Seller under the Asset Purchase Agreement, Guarantor will immediately make such payments.

IN WITNESS WHEREOF, the undersigned has executed this Guaranty under seal on this 30th day of December YR-3.

GUARANTOR:

Arthur Dillon

Arthur Dillon

SEAL

Personal Financial Statement Date of Statement: March 23, YR-3

Name (first, middle, last) Arthur R. Dillon	Birth date 4-1-YR-48	Phone number (212) 555-1212		Social security number 468-24-xxxx
Home address (include apt.) 540 8th Street	City, state, zip New York, NY 10004			How long? 20 years
If joint statement, list joint applicant financial information: N/A			Social security number of joint party:	

Assets S= single J = joint	Value	Liabilities	Loan Amount	Credit Limit	Monthly payment	Balance
Cash on hand, & unrestricted in banks (Mo. market, checking, CDs)	$ 825,000	Notes payable to banks	N/A			$ 825,000
Cash surrender value life insurance	$ 5,000,000	Loans against life ins.	($1,000,000)			$4,000,000
Retirement accounts (401K, IRA, etc.)		Loans against ret. accts.	N/A			
Listed (NYSE, AMEX) stocks, bonds		Margin loans				
		Credit cards	No balance carried			
Real estate (primary residence) New York	$ 2,000,000	Mortgage/rent (primary residence)	N/A			$2,000,000
Real estate (secondary residence) Arizona	$ 1,775,000	Mortgage (secondary residence)	N/A			$1,775,000
		Home equity loans	N/A			
Vehicles Mercedes Benz, Lexus	$ 100,000	Vehicle loans/ leases	N/A			$ 100,000
Notes/Accounts receivable		Taxes accrued but unpaid	N/A			
Other assets (describe) Dynamo Sporting Goods—Owner	$19,000,000	Other liabilities (describe) Mortgage, inventory financing, equip. loans	($12,700,000)		$ 14,568	$6,300,000
		Contingent Liabilities As guarantor or co-maker, Legal claims on leases or contracts	N/A			
TOTAL ASSETS	$28,700,000	TOTAL LIABILITIES	($13,700,000)	NET WORTH (assets minus liabilities)		$15 million

Income Information __Monthly _X_Annual Alimony, child support or separate maintenance income need not be listed.		Banking Relationships (Deposits only) Bank Name	S=Single J=Joint	Cash Balance
Gross salary, wages, tips	$600,000	First National Bank of Nita		$825,000
Bonus/commissions (recurring)	350,000			
Other income (dividends, interest, etc.)	100,000			
TOTAL INCOME	$1,050,000	TOTAL CASH		$825,000

This financial statement is submitted as a separate attachment to my credit application. I warrant that there is no judgment against me nor lien unsatisfied upon my property except as shown, nor prior suit pending against me in any court, that no assets are pledged in any manner herein, and that this statement is true and complete and is offered for the purpose of obtaining and maintaining credit. With joint credit, all applicants must sign.

arthur Dillon   March 23, YR-3

Personal Financial Statement Date of Statement: December 23, YR-3

Name (first, middle, last) **Arthur R. Dillon**	Birth date **4-1-YR-48**	Phone number **(212) 555-1212**		Social security number **468-24-xxxx**
Home address (include apt.) **540 8th Street**	City, state, zip **New York, NY 10004**			How long? **20 years**

If joint statement, list joint applicant financial information: N/A		Social security number of joint party:

Assets S= single J = joint	**Value**	**Liabilities**	**Loan Amount**	**Credit Limit**	**Monthly payment**	**Balance**
Cash on hand, & unrestricted in banks **(Mo. market, checking, CDs)**	$ 825,000	Notes payable to banks	N/A			$ 825,000
Cash surrender value life insurance	$ 5,000,000	Loans against life ins.	($1,000,000)			$4,000,000
Retirement accounts (401K, IRA, etc.)		Loans against ret. accts.	N/A			
Listed (NYSE, AMEX) stocks, bonds		Margin loans				
		Credit cards	No balance carried			
Real estate (primary residence) **New York**	$ 2,000,000	Mortgage/rent (primary residence)	N/A			$2,000,000
Real estate (secondary residence) **Arizona**	$ 1,775,000	Mortgage (secondary residence)	N/A			$1,775,000
		Home equity loans	N/A			
Vehicles **Mercedes Benz, Lexus**	$ 100,000	Vehicle loans/ leases	N/A			$ 100,000
Notes/Accounts receivable		Taxes accrued but unpaid	N/A			
Other assets (describe) **Dynamo Sporting Goods—Owner**	$19,000,000	Other liabilities (describe) **Mortgage, inventory financing, equip. loans**	($12,700,000)		$ 14,568	$6,300,000
		Contingent Liabilities As guarantor or co-maker, Legal claims on leases or contracts	N/A			
TOTAL ASSETS	**$28,700,000**	**TOTAL LIABILITIES**	**($13,700,000)**	**NET WORTH** (assets minus liabilities)		**$15 million**

Income Information __Monthly _X_ Annual Alimony, child support or separate maintenance income need not be listed.		Banking Relationships (Deposits only) Bank Name S=Single J=Joint		Cash Balance
Gross salary, wages, tips	$600,000	**First National Bank of Nita**		**$825,000**
Bonus/commissions (recurring)	350,000			
Other income (dividends, interest, etc.)	100,000			
TOTAL INCOME	**$1,050,000**	**TOTAL CASH**		**$825,000**

This financial statement is submitted as a separate attachment to my credit application. I warrant that there is no judgment against me nor lien unsatisfied upon my property except as shown, nor prior suit pending against me in any court, that no assets are pledged in any manner herein, and that this statement is true and complete and is offered for the purpose of obtaining and maintaining credit. With joint credit, all applicants must sign.

arthur Dillon

12-23-YR-3

MATERIALS FOR A'S

REPRESENTING MICHELLE PAUL

STATEMENTS AND CORRESPONDENCE

STATEMENTS OF PARTIES AND WITNESSES

STATEMENT OF MICHELLE PAUL

I started Sportslifeware in YR-7 to manufacture and sell sportswear for women. I was thirty-five years old and had worked in the fashion industry since high school, doing it full time after graduating from the MBA program at Emory in YR-18. After working in several jobs involving production and marketing, I decided to try to start my own company, Sportslifeware. Yes, I was young, but I had a lot of ideas and had made some good connections. By April of YR-7, I developed a business plan and had secured start-up financing. Yes, I was employed by a company in Nita City when I sought financing. No, I didn't tell them what I was doing, but I did it on my own time. I was able to get into production by late summer, YR-7. At first, I did not own my manufacturing facility; I contracted with other companies to produce my products. But quality control is critical for the high-end market, and I quickly became dissatisfied with the quality of the work my suppliers produced.

By early summer of YR-6, I had acquired the last three years of a lease on a small manufacturing facility in Dalton, Georgia, a small city near Atlanta. Spandau, the company that had been leasing the facility, was shutting down all of its U.S. manufacturing operations and moving them to Malaysia. Because Spandau was eager to cut its losses in the U.S., I negotiated a sublease with Spandau agreeing to pay half of the remaining lease payments. It was a great deal for me.

Once I took direct control over production, the quality of my products increased dramatically, and so did sales. Sportslifeware made substantial profits in both YR-5 and YR-4. Despite this success, during the holidays in December YR-4, I decided to sell my business. No one thing initially led to this decision. It was a perfect storm, I guess. The manufacturing lease was ending, and I had been working 24/7 to make the company successful, but the excitement was gone. I felt "burned out" after working three years to make the company successful.

I was also getting tired of the same challenges that retail brought and was beginning to think that I could be even more successful doing something more cutting edge, like an e-business. No, I didn't have any plans to do anything then. In January YR-3, I announced my intentions to sell at the industrywide trade show in Atlanta and my announcement generated some interest. I had telephone conversations with a couple of people. No, I don't remember who they were. None of them seemed like serious buyers to me, and I was not going to turn over the business I worked so hard to create to someone who would run it into the ground. Ironic, isn't it?

Yes, I was concerned that the end of my lease would impact the profitability of my business, at least to the extent we had recently enjoyed. Despite the higher labor costs in the United States, I had competed successfully with foreign producers because the sublease negotiated with Spandau dramatically reduced production costs; that offset some of the labor cost advantage for foreign manufacturers. When the existing lease expired at the end of YR-3, I knew my costs would go up. To preserve my manufacturing capability, in late YR-4, I was in protracted negotiations for a new five-year lease, to take effect on January 1, YR-2. Even though that lease was still somewhat favorable to me, it increased my lease payments by another 30 percent. This increase in costs was going to force me to raise prices. I would be either on a level playing field or even at a disadvantage with some of my competitors. As a result, I determined that YR-3 might be the best year to sell my business. Sportslifeware had a good track record of profitability in the previous three years, but increased costs might change the balance sheet dramatically.

Yes, it's true that I talked to potential buyers about the customer list that I developed as an asset of Sportslifeware. It was a unique list of customers and potential customers for specialty, high-end women's sportswear. I considered the customer list valuable because it gave me an advantage over my competitors and everyone knew it. Yes, I started creating the list when I worked at Womensport, my last job before starting Sportslifeware. At Womensport, I was in charge of trying to develop new customers. In doing so, I had the idea of putting together a list of exclusive clothing stores. Some were well-known retailers, like Neiman Marcus, but the great majority were small, independent stores and shops located throughout the United States and in Canada and the Caribbean. I created and produced the initial list by calling my personal contacts in the industry, and by researching on Google and in trade publications. The information I developed provided the basis for the list we used at Sportslifeware. I refined it by continually researching trade publications, scouring phone listings in exclusive towns and cities, and personally calling every lead I developed. It took me almost a year to complete this work. Of course, I understood that it was valuable, which is why I worked so hard on it. I suppose I knew that the list was a significant business asset, because few if any other producers of high-end specialty fashions would have such a complete list of potential customers, let alone have made personal contact with virtually all of them. Completing this list was one of the reasons I decided to leave Womensport and to start Sportslifeware. Yes, I did show potential lenders this list when I was shopping for start-up financing for Sportslifeware. The bankers all seemed to think it gave me a competitive advantage. Yes, they used those words, I think.

No, Womensport did not give me permission to take the list when I left. It was my work alone, used only by me when I worked at Womensport. I am not sure anyone else at Womensport even knew that I had developed it, used it, or that it even existed. It was on my computer only, used solely by me. I emailed the list to my home computer, even before I left Womensport. I often worked from home on it, so I emailed it back and forth several times as it grew. I did not have a confidentiality agreement with Womensport. No, I didn't have any employment agreement, either, at least not that I remember.

When I started Sportslifeware, I continued developing the list, with the assistance of J.J. Lyons. It was a very good list by YR-3 because of the amount of additional work we put into it. No, I can't estimate how much of the list was done at Womensport and how much at Sportslifeware. A list like that is a continually evolving process. No, I didn't keep it under lock and key, but it was safeguarded at Sportslifeware. J.J. Lyons ran the Sales Department, and we did have employment agreements with the sales staff. He made sure that people had it only on a need-to-know basis. Only J.J. and the sales staff had access to the list, and he monitored who had the list. Of course, I had it, too. Yes, it was on our computers, but they all are password protected. No, I don't think the list has a personal and confidential watermark on it. At least my copy didn't.

I talked to Arthur Dillon sometime after meeting him at the industry trade show. He was the first person who seemed to have a plan for developing and running Sportslifeware that made sense. Dillon wanted to integrate it into what he described as other sports companies, as a natural expansion. He already had a manufacturing plant that could be retooled to do our manufacturing, so the lease issue didn't bother him. It seemed like a good fit. I was eager to meet with him in March in New York, and celebrated by treating myself to a weekend of skiing over the President's Day Holiday. Unfortunately, I fell and broke my femur. I had to have surgery and couldn't travel. Instead, Dillon came to Atlanta to see me at the end of March. I don't have my calendar here, but March 24 sounds right.

The negotiations with Dillon went quickly, and within an hour or so, we had agreed upon a deal. Our only real discussion was about the fact that he couldn't come up with a substantial amount as a down payment, and wanted to pay even less than 10 percent down. He told me that he was involved in extensive equipment purchases for his other companies and was very cash poor in YR-3. Stupidly, I agreed to those terms, but I did insist on a personal guaranty. A lot of good that did, right? He told me he'd be glad to sign one, and he had a current financial statement to back it up. He had that document faxed or scanned to my office, and I looked at it. Since we conducted the negotiations in my office, I typed up the terms of what I thought of was our "intent to agree" agreement on my computer, and we signed it. Dillon was able to catch an early flight back to New York.

Why did we agree so quickly? Well, after the accident, I was exhausted. That added to my desire to get out and let someone else deal with leases and production schedules. Dillon was also the only real potential buyer that could deal with the manufacturing issues. I should have known I wasn't functioning on all cylinders at that time.

When we met, Dillon did tell me that the customer list was one of the things he wanted to purchase. Yes, he may have said he considered the list to be one of the company's key proprietary assets. But he was only parroting the information that I had talked about at the trade shows. He had never seen the list and didn't know if it was valuable or not. I didn't put an exact price on it, no. I don't know if the accountants did when they conducted an audit before I sold Sportslifeware, but I wasn't aware of any cash value put on it. No, I didn't look at the audit before closing. It was up to the buyer to do that, wasn't it?

Because I was dealing with a company in Nita City, I hired Jamie Norris to represent me. Norris had done a good job when representing me in earlier deals there, and I thought that using a Nita City lawyer might expedite closing the deal, particularly since Dillon said his lawyer was nearby, in Connecticut. During our negotiations, Dillon told me that his lawyer, Sam Hanson, had represented him in all of his business and financial dealings for years. Dillon specifically told me Hanson could finalize the deal faster than anyone else. I remember specifically what he said: "Hanson knows my business and finances better than anyone."

It turned out that the deal did not close quickly, but the delay was not my lawyer's fault. The lawyers had finalized the paperwork for the agreement by July of YR-3, but for reasons that I didn't understand at the time, Dillon delayed the closing until the last possible moment. I have since learned that Dillon was in financial trouble, and I believe that he simply couldn't come up with the money required to close the deal.

As the months passed and my injuries healed, it's true that I began to regret my decision to get out of the business. The longer that Dillon delayed the closing, the more I realized I wasn't ready to completely leave the business. In fact, as I wondered if he was going to be able to come to closing, I realized that if he couldn't close the deal, I might be happy to continue running Sportslifeware, despite the impending increase in production costs. But Jamie Norris kept reassuring me that the deal would close.

After yet another postponement of the closing, I began planning a new company I could start after the sale of Sportslifeware. If the deal with Dillon didn't close, the plan was a blueprint for the metamorphosis of Sportslifeware. I realized that I loved women's sportswear and that I could use the sale of my business as an opportunity to move directly into e-commerce. No, I wasn't going to open the exact same business. I wanted to create a very different business model for my new company, one that would take advantage of the emergence of business-to-business commerce. The new company would not manufacture the product line. We would design the products and then have them manufactured elsewhere, where manufacturing costs were lower than in the United States. It was completely different from anything I had ever done, and it excited me.

To further hold down costs, I envisioned that the new company would minimize its role in receiving, storing, and distributing its products. We would use internet technology to receive orders from customers and then pass those orders to the company's suppliers. The suppliers would ship the products directly to the customers who had ordered them. My goal was to provide unprecedented flexibility and speed in filling customer orders while holding costs to an absolute minimum. Because of my success with Sportslifeware and my innovative business model for the new company, I was able to secure start-up funding by Thanksgiving of YR-3.

I didn't solicit any employees. When I first started thinking about this e-business concept, I did talk to some of my best employees to ask them if they were interested in working for me. Those conversations were in the summer and fall of YR-3, when Dillon kept postponing the closing and I wasn't sure if the sale would actually close. I would have used that concept either on Sportslifeware or started an entirely new business. The two employees that I most wanted were J.J. Lyons, Director of Sales and Marketing, and Sal Duane, Director of Production. They were my most talented, most productive employees. Although both decided that they would stay with Sportslifeware if it sold, I told them they always could have a job with me. Both were concerned about leaving the security of a successful company for the unknown of a new and risky startup. I understood. I couldn't guarantee them that the new company would last.

Ultimately, however, the deal closed. The closing was in December in Nita City. At the closing, Dillon produced a cashier's check for $500,000. As I said, this was considerably less than 10 percent of the purchase price, and ordinarily I would not have agreed to such a small down payment, but when we negotiated the deal in March I was sick, exhausted, and just too eager to sell.

You need to understand that Dillon's personal guaranty was particularly important to me, precisely because the down payment was so small. Without it, I would never have closed the deal. I really believed that Dillon had more than enough personal assets to cover the $5.5 million due the following September. The agreement we worked out required that he have at least $13 million in personal assets at the time of closing or I could walk away from the deal. At the closing, Dillon's attorney, Sam Hanson, included in the closing documents an updated financial statement showing that Dillon still had a net worth of more than $15 million. At the time, I was actually disappointed, although I didn't say so. I would have been happy not to close the deal. Based on what I've learned since the closing, however, I now believe that the financial statement Dillon submitted at the closing was false. No, I didn't examine it in detail at the closing. Of course, I didn't compare it to the first financial statement I got. Why should I? Sorry, but for one thing, I didn't have the March statement at the closing. For another, we had Dillon's lawyer personally preparing and reviewing all the closing documents. He wrote my lawyer an email saying he was doing everything himself. Why would I think they weren't on the up and up?

By mid-January YR-2, my new company, "Sportique Sportswear for Life," was up and running. I was lucky to have plenty of startup financing, because the company lost money during the initial months. One problem was marketing. Because I had sold my customer list to Dillon, I was forced to try and reconstruct that list. This was possible, of course. I had done it once before and much of the information I needed was available from public sources like the phone book, the internet, trade publications, and so forth. But when I originally created the list at Womensport, I had lots more time. I wasn't running a brand new company. Now most of my time was devoted to starting and running a new company, with new employees, and I had relatively little time to devote to the effort it would take to recreate the list. I needed someone who could take charge of this project.

J.J. Lyons and I continued our friendship after the company sold. We met occasionally for coffee and drinks to catch up. Sometime in February YR-2, when J.J. and I were having a drink, we talked about my continuing search for a Director of Sales. At that point, J.J. said that staying with Sportslifeware had been a mistake. J.J. asked to apply for the job at Sportique. We discussed terms; I offered salary and a percentage of the company's profits. No, I wouldn't call it soliciting another company's employee. I just wanted the best for J.J. Yes, it was good for me and my new company, too. After several phone conversations and a meeting or two, J.J. came to work for Sportique in mid-March of YR-2.

Did I go back and read the Asset Purchase Agreement between closing and when J.J. came to work for me? No, I don't remember doing so. Did I believe I agreed not to hire any Sportique employees? Ever? Under any circumstances? No. What I did was hire a friend who wanted to work for me instead of working for Dillon. No court would order J.J. Lyons to work for Dillon, would they?

Of course, J.J. knew how valuable the customer list could be to the new company. We both knew how we had developed it and used it. I mentioned that I was trying to recreate it and how much time it was taking me. But I never asked J.J. to steal the list from Sportslifeware. Never once did I say take it, bring it, or anything like that. Yes, J.J. came to work in March with the customer list on a laptop. I don't remember our exact conversation, but evidently the list was just floating around Sportslifeware after Dillon took over and people had it who shouldn't have. In essence, J.J. couldn't stand to see all that hard work not being appreciated and being handled so carelessly by Dillon. And then J.J. told me that rumors were flying at Sportslifeware that Dillon was running the company into the ground. J.J. was afraid that the list would be lost in a bankruptcy proceeding, and couldn't stand to see that happen. Frankly that thought made me sick.

Yes, once we started using the list, we were able to spend our time directly on marketing rather than identifying customers. Within weeks, Sportique was getting orders from Sportslifeware's old customers and within three or four months, we had gotten orders from almost 60 percent of the businesses on the old customer list.

Before J.J. arrived, Sportique had another problem. Because our products were being manufactured by other companies in other countries, it was critically important that the company have the ability to monitor and direct the production activities of these other manufacturers. Unfortunately, I had been unable to hire a production director who could really make this happen.

When J.J. came over to Sportique, Sal Duane also agreed to be the Director of Production for Sportique. Okay, we talked, but the decision to leave Sportslifeware was entirely Sal's. Yes, I offered a compensation package similar to the one I gave to Lyons. At the time, I thought that it was money well-spent. Because of Sal's knowledge of clothing manufacturing, Sal was able to help the suppliers improve their production and inspection methods, and the quality problems that had plagued our early products were largely eliminated. As a result, when my old customers began to get their shipments, they were pleased with the quality and ordered more. Sportique has been profitable since the third quarter of our first year.

Unfortunately, right after Thanksgiving, Sal demanded a huge pay raise, including a significant increase in profit percentage. Sal claimed to have saved the company and deserved to be compensated for it. I refused, because I had already broken the bank to hire Lyons and Duane in the first place, and could not afford to give any raises. Sal got angry and quit. I do not know where Sal's is working now. We have had no contact since then.

Losing Sal Duane because I couldn't afford to pay more made me realize that I needed to pursue the $5.5 million Dillon owed me for the purchase of Sportslifeware as soon as possible. Dillon had failed to make the balloon payment due in September YR-2. I didn't go after it as aggressively as I should have right away, because I was so busy with Sportique. Starting in January YR-1, I think, I called Dillon repeatedly, and left messages with strong demands for payment. No, I didn't get lawyers involved at first because I thought that I could handle it myself. Dillon stonewalled me at first, but later said that he owed me nothing, because I had supposedly breached our agreement first. That was when I decided I would have to sue him to recover the money he owed me.

I attest that I have read the foregoing and that it is true and correct to the best of my knowledge, information, and belief.

Michelle Paul
_____
Michelle Paul

STATEMENT OF J.J. LYONS

I am currently the Director of Sales and Marketing for Sportique. I went to work for Michelle Paul's prior company, Sportslifeware, when Michelle started it in YR-7. Before that, I worked in marketing for various companies. But despite my success in every job, I was working in large corporations and never rose to a Director of Sales position. Because Michelle was building Sportslifeware from scratch, she was willing to take a gamble on me. The chance to be in charge of sales was enough to get me to jump into a new company.

I think Michelle Paul did an incredible job of building Sportslifeware. In particular, she had a real knack for finding talented people to design her products, manage production and distribution. She was not a micromanager, and allowed her managers to take a lot of initiative. Yes, I did contribute to Sportlifeware's success. I did a very good job of selling and marketing their products. My job was made much easier by the fact that Michelle provided me with a list of current and potential customers that she had developed at her previous job. How do I know that? She told me. She said when she was working at Womensport, it was her idea to develop that kind of specialized list. It was entirely her work product. I don't remember when or where we talked about that, but I just knew it.

Even when I first saw it, that list was remarkable in scope. What do I mean? Well, Michelle had identified many of the retail outlets for high-end women's sportswear in North America and the Caribbean, including businesses in locations that most companies would never target. In addition, the customer list contained incredible detail, not just each business's address and telephone number, but also information about the people who ran each business, an analysis of each business's history, and demographic information about the customers in the business's market locale. The list was invaluable, and a big part of my job as Director of Sales was to build on it, and to keep the information we already had updated to reflect changes in both our customers and our business over time. No, I don't keep time records in my job, but I would estimate that 30 percent of my time at Sportslifeware might have been spent on the list. I was not only updating it, but getting new businesses added and then cold calling and researching the details that made the list important.

Things went well at Sportslifeware until the holiday break in YR-4. When Michelle returned to work after only a few days off, it seemed like the stress was getting to her. She had the stress of the lease negotiations with the manufacturing plant, the long hours, and the constant pressures of this business. In February YR-3, when she took a much-needed vacation, Michelle had a bad skiing accident and had to have surgery. After she got out of the hospital, she seemed to have lost all interest in the business, and only a few weeks later, word spread through the company that she was planning on selling. Near the end of March, Michelle announced to the employees that she had signed an intent to sell the company during YR-3. She emphasized that although the buyer was from New York, he planned to keep producing the same product line in Georgia.

YR-3 was a struggle for the company. Everyone was anxious about the change in management; we kept waiting for the sale to occur in July, then later in the summer, but it was delayed for months, until the very end of December. The delay was really bad for morale.

Sometime in the fall of YR-3, before the sale closed, Michelle became frustrated and unsure whether the sale would go through. She told me that she had decided to either revamp Sportslifeware or start a new company called Sportique. It would produce sportswear like the products we had been selling. In either event, she wanted me to be Director of Sales. Yes, it could have been September, I don't remember. No, I don't have records from that time. I don't keep stuff like that in my calendar.

I thought about it for a few days, but told her if Sportslifeware sold, I'd stay with them. I knew the new owner wanted me. I had some doubts about the business plan for Michelle's new company, particularly the idea of having all product manufacturing outsourced and then delivered directly to the customer without being handled and inspected by Sportique. In addition, I knew that the customer list was included in the sale of the business, and I was a little concerned about trying to create it again. It would be possible to reproduce much of the information in the list, but it would probably take a year or more of hard work to do it, and some of the information inevitably would be lost. I didn't look forward to the prospect of trying to sell new products in competition with a company that already had all the information that we'd spent a lot of time to develop.

Shortly after Arthur Dillon took over Sportslifeware, I started to think I'd made a mistake in not joining Michelle at Sportique. Dillon not only seemed uninterested in the company, he seemed strapped for cash. As far as anyone could tell, he did not put any of the company's profits back into the company. Instead of improving Sportslifeware, Dillon seemed bent on taking every dollar he could out of it. Word began to circulate in the company that Dillon was not even keeping current on paying the company's bills, which was a big change from the way Michelle had run things. There was even gossip that Dillon was not only close to filing bankruptcy, but that he had been in that kind of financial trouble since the summer of YR-3, and the only thing that was keeping him afloat was the cash generated by Sportslifeware.

I ignored the gossip until an event that made me believe that the rumors could be true. In late January YR-2, my assistant Pat Hingle and I had a lunch meeting with Gerry Jackson, Comptroller for Sportslifeware. The meeting was just to get to know each other. Jackson arrived late and seemed really uptight. We accomplished almost nothing at the meeting because Jackson spent the entire lunch drinking scotch and complaining about the company's finances. What do I mean by complaining? Well, after his second or third drink, he started telling us that Dillon was bleeding the company's accounts dry. Yes, I think those were the words he used. I remember that Jackson said that we should watch out, because Dillon could drive the company into the ground. He said that Dillon had done the same thing with his first company, Dynamo Sport, and the only reason that Dynamo Sport could pay its bills was that Dillon had been using his personal assets for the last six months to support the company. I remember asking him how much money he was talking about. Jackson said something like, "Well, it's not peanuts. It's way up in the six figures, probably in the seven figures." Yes, those were his words. Hingle and I both looked at each other and it was clear we were pretty shocked.

By February, I had become increasingly nervous about the company's future. Sometime during that month, Michelle called me. We had kept in touch since the sale, just catching up on personal stuff over drinks and coffee. Her enthusiasm over what she was doing was very attractive. And my frustration and unhappiness must have showed. Michelle was still looking for a Director of Sales. I asked her if I could apply for the job. She said she would welcome me back and give me a stake in the company. Although I was still reluctant to leave for a start-up, the ever increasing negative gossip was undermining my confidence. In February, we had a couple of other phone conversations and meetings. I also told her about the rumors that Dillon was running Sportslifeware into the ground. We both discussed how awful it would be if the list were lost in a bankruptcy proceeding. I couldn't stand to see the thought of all that work going to waste.

Did I take the customer list? I want to be clear about this. I didn't steal it or take it for the purpose of giving it to Michelle Paul. I had the list on my personal laptop when Michelle ran Sportslifeware and when Dillon bought it. I had to have it accessible because I often needed to work from home to reach customers in different time zones. But I did continue to use it when I got to Sportique. I didn't think I was doing anything illegal, no. But it did make me a little uncomfortable, because I knew Dillon bought the list. The bottom line is that I couldn't stand seeing all the hard work that Michelle and I had done go to waste. Dillon didn't care about the list. If Dillon drove Sportslifeware into the ground, the list was no good to anyone.

Yes, both Michelle and Dillon repeatedly told Sportslifeware employees that they had to be careful with the list. Our computers were password protected and Dillon told us never to show the list to anyone outside the Sales and Marketing team unless it was absolutely necessary. Yes, everyone involved in sales and management at Sportslifeware recognized that the customer list was an asset for the company. Everyone in sales relied on it. Dillon even told us not to take the list outside of the company offices. I thought this was pretty unrealistic, however, because there were copies of the list on thumb drives and printed hard copies, and Hingle and I had to use the list outside of the office if we were to do our jobs. Because many of our customers were in different time zones, we contacted them at night or on weekends. I have to believe Michelle Paul and Arthur Dillon both knew we were working from home, and so we had to be using the list outside the office, but I didn't have that conversation with either of them. No, unlike with Michelle, Dillon never required me to sign an employment contract or other written agreement promising to keep the customer list confidential and secret. Yes, I knew it would be important to keep it confidential, with or without a written agreement.

Did Michelle ever tell me to take the list and give it to her? No. she didn't. Yes, we talked about the list more than once. During my February conversations with Michelle, we talked a lot about the success we had, how creative and innovative the list was, and how Dillon didn't have the imagination to understand what it was worth. I think she regretted that she included the list in the sale. What did she say? Just that she wished she hadn't sold the list. We talked about reconstructing the list. Much of the information in it could eventually be found from public sources or reconstructed from memory, if we could put the time into it. But the problem was the time it would take, since we both forecasted that initial sales of Sportique's products would be slow, and we could anticipate some production problems. We knew the company might not survive without a quick uptick in sales.

Sal Duane came to Sportique at about the same time I did. Sal did the same great job as always with the production side of things, and the improved product quality combined with my sales and marketing efforts produced an almost immediate effect. Before the end of second quarter, sales were up, and they were up dramatically before the end of YR-2. It looked as if the company would not only survive, but would grow and prosper. Sure, that benefited me directly. Yes, I told you I have a profit-sharing arrangement. Unfortunately, near the end of YR-2, Michelle and Duane had a disagreement about money, and Sal quit in a huff. I don't know if or where Sal is working now.

I attest that I have read the foregoing and that it is true and correct to the best of my knowledge, information, and belief.

J.J. Lyons

J.J. Lyons

MEMO

To:	The File—Witness Interview Notes
From:	Donald Davis
Subject:	**Michelle Paul v. Dynamo, et al.**
	Phone call from Donald Davis to Sal Duane, former Director of Production for Sportslifeware and Sportique Clothing
Date:	February 14, YR-1

Located Duane through Client, Michelle Paul. Reached Duane at home. Identified myself, told Duane of litigation between client and defendants. When I explained why I was calling, Duane actually laughed. When I inquired why the laughter, Duane said:

> *"I worked for both Paul and Dillon and they treated me terribly. One was a liar, and the other a thief. I'm not going to say anything that could help either of them, and I'm not going to talk to you. Do not call or contact me again."*

Duane terminated the conversation.

CORRESPONDENCE

Michelle Paul

From:	Jamie Norris, Proskow & Proskow, Attorneys at Law <jamie@proskow.nita>
Sent:	June 12, YR-3
To:	Michelle Paul <mpaul@sportslifeware.nita>
Subject:	*NOTICE*: THIS E-MAIL MESSAGE IS A CONFIDENTIAL ATTORNEY-CLIENT COMMUNICATION

Michelle,

Art Dillon's attorney just sent me what I believe will be the final version of the closing documents for the sale of your company. As I told you on the telephone, he and I completed the negotiations of the final terms last week. Given the nature of the agreement that you and Dillon signed back in March, I think the payment terms are as good as we can get. Dillon will sign a personal guarantee, and you won't have to sell unless he can verify a personal net worth of $13 million dollars.

Sam Hanson, Dillon's lawyer, is getting ready to leave on vacation and asked if we could postpone the closing until he returns. I agreed. That will give each of us time to go over the documents carefully, to make sure that you are satisfied. Hanson promised to communicate with his client before he leaves, so we can have the closing as soon as Hanson returns from vacation. As you know, Dillon has been eager to finish the deal, so I think we can anticipate finalizing things in July.

You should receive a copy of the documents by tomorrow. Call me if you have any questions.

Michelle Paul

From:	Michelle Paul <mpaul@sportslifeware.nita>
Sent:	July 22, YR-3
To:	Jamie Norris, Proskow & Proskow, Attorneys at Law <jamie@proskow.nita>
Subject:	Re: ***NOTICE***: THIS E-MAIL MESSAGE IS A CONFIDENTIAL ATTORNEY-CLIENT COMMUNICATION

I am very frustrated. I know it is not your fault, but I am becoming increasingly concerned that Dillon is not financially sound and won't be able to close. And even if he can come up with the $500,000 I stupidly agreed to take as a down, what if he stiffs me on the rest? I know he looks OK, but I'm worried. He said that Sam Hanson handles everything for him and you said you trusted Hanson. Can you get Hanson to assure us that Dillon is on the up and up?

I am getting very nervous about this whole deal……

From:	Jamie Norris, Proskow & Proskow, Attorneys at Law <jamie@proskow.nita>
Sent:	July 22, YR-3
To:	Michelle Paul <mpaul@sportslifeware.nita>
Subject:	***NOTICE***: THIS E-MAIL MESSAGE IS A CONFIDENTIAL ATTORNEY-CLIENT COMMUNICATION

Michelle,

I just got off the telephone with Dillon's attorney, Sam Hanson, and I wanted to keep you up to date on these conversations. As you know, I've spoken with Hanson several times over the past three weeks. I told him that you had second thoughts about the sale and Dillon's financial condition. I said that you were willing to walk away from the MOA. Hanson assured me that Dillon would meet the terms of the agreement.

However, I get the definite impression that he, or his client, is stalling for some reason, which is surprising since Hanson has been telling me for four months that his client wants to close the deal ASAP. When I asked Hanson why he and his client had not picked a date for the closing, he was evasive. I did not get any indication that Dillon was trying to back out of the deal. Hanson specifically said that Dillon would have the $500,000 required at the closing. When we were negotiating the terms of the Asset Purchase Agreement back in the late spring and early summer, Hanson told me that he handled all of Dillon's legal affairs and all of his personal and business financial transactions. As Dillon told you, Hanson reaffirmed that he is intimately familiar with Dillon's and Dynamo's finances. I know that he has a lot of influence with Dillon, and he specifically told me that he would review all of the closing documents himself to ensure they were fine. At the end of the conversation, Hanson promised to call Dillon and try to move this deal along, so hopefully we will get some results in the near future.

I know that the delays are beginning to cause you some frustration and concern, but the Agreement allows Dillon to wait until the end of the year to finalize the purchase and sale of your business. You might as well try to make the best of things, and leave the worrying to me.

Michelle Paul

From:	Jamie Norris, Proskow & Proskow, Attorneys at Law <jamie@proskow.nita>
Sent:	September 19, YR-3
To:	Michelle Paul <mpaul@sportslifeware.nita>
Subject:	***NOTICE***: THIS E-MAIL MESSAGE IS A CONFIDENTIAL ATTORNEY-CLIENT COMMUNICATION

Michelle,

Just an update on the Dillon deal. I have called Dillon's attorney several times over the past two weeks, and he has not returned my phone calls. I know you said you are worried about Dillon backing out. I do not have any more information than I did last month. Don't worry; I'm persistent.

Michelle Paul

From:	Jamie Norris, Proskow & Proskow, Attorneys at Law <jamie@proskow.nita>
Sent:	November 11, YR-3
To:	Michelle Paul<mpaul@sportslifeware.nita>
Subject:	***NOTICE***: THIS E-MAIL MESSAGE IS A CONFIDENTIAL ATTORNEY-CLIENT COMMUNICATION

Michelle,

I received a phone call from Sam Hanson today. He suggested—without specifying a date—that Dillon does not want to close before the very end of December. I don't know if you will think this is progress or not, and he did not tell me what, if anything, has changed.

Michelle, I know that you are having serious second thoughts about selling your business, and reservations about whether Dillon is the right buyer. I have expressed those concerns to Hanson. Let me remind you that the MOA that you typed and signed last March gives Dillon every right to take this long to close. As long as he is able to pay $500,000 at closing and proves he has sufficient personal worth at closing, he will not have breached the agreement. Once a final closing date is set, I'll let you know. Be patient.

Michelle Paul

From:	Jamie Norris, Proskow & Proskow, Attorneys at Law <jamie@proskow.nita>
Sent:	November 19, YR-3
To:	Michelle Paul<mpaul@sportslifeware.nita>
Subject:	***NOTICE***: THIS E-MAIL MESSAGE IS A CONFIDENTIAL ATTORNEY-CLIENT COMMUNICATION

Michelle,

In your email of yesterday, you asked about hiring current employees for the new company. As you know, the Asset Purchase Agreement between you and Dillon contains standard language saying that you will not try to hire Sportslifeware employees, compete for customers, take trade secrets, etc., etc., etc., for three years after the closing.

If the deal doesn't close, then you can do whatever you want. If the deal closes, you can still do whatever you want, but to be frank, it could lead to litigation. If it does lead to litigation, there is no way to know for certain how things will turn out. Nita courts may enforce those kinds of contract restrictions, but they haven't always, if they feel they are unfair. The facts of each case would be critical. In either event, you would be faced with the expense and aggravation of litigation if Dillon decided to sue, right at the time all your efforts should be devoted to your new company.

I hope you have a great Thanksgiving holiday.

From:	Michelle Paul <mpaul@sportslifeware.nita>
Sent:	November 18, YR-3
To:	Jamie Norris, Proskow & Proskow, Attorneys at Law <jamie@proskow.nita>
Subject:	

Jamie,

I am writing to get some advice about how to handle the new company I am starting. As you know, after the sale of Sportslifeware (assuming that this actually will happen), I will be in a position to start a new company. My goal is to take advantage of new technologies to manufacture clothing overseas and distribute it directly to my customers. This is a sophisticated concept, and I will need the best people in the business to pull it off. In particular, production will have to be managed perfectly, or I'll get destroyed in terms of product quality and delivery on schedule issues. I also will need a great sales director to persuade my old customers to take a chance on this new kind of distribution model. Right now, I have two of the best people in the business in charge of production and sales. Is there any reason I can't take them with me? I've told them about my plans and told them that there would be positions for them in the new company, but I wanted to run it by you before we finalize.

If you could get back to me about this ASAP, it would be helpful. Have a great Thanksgiving.

Michelle

Michelle Paul

From:	Jamie Norris, Proskow & Proskow, Attorneys at Law <jamie@proskow.nita>
Sent:	December 29, YR-3
To:	Michelle Paul<mpaul@sportslifeware.nita>
Subject:	FWD: Closing: Sportslifeware Acquisition ***NOTICE***: THIS E-MAIL MESSAGE IS A CONFIDENTIAL ATTORNEY-CLIENT COMMUNICATION

Michelle,

Earlier today I spoke with Sam Hanson to confirm that things are set for the closing tomorrow. As you know, most of the closing documents were finished some time ago. There are some last-minute things for the closing, however, like Dillon's updated financial statement, which Hanson says he is sending over by courier today. Hanson said that he thought everything was fine, and the closing should be smooth and quick. Again he promised that because of the long delay, rather than follow his standard practice of having an associate or paralegal do the final file review, he has gone over all of the closing documents himself. I told him that I was especially worried about the financial statement, but he assured me that it was fine. Because of the problems we have had with delays, I asked Hanson to send me an email confirming the same. I just received that email. I am forwarding it with this message so you could see that we are, in fact, going to close this deal. Do you want to see the documents today, or come in tomorrow to review them? Let me know.

I look forward to seeing you tomorrow.

Attached is the email from Hanson:

FROM:	samhanson@DHLlaw.nita
TO:	Jamie Norris, Proskow & Proskow, Attorneys at Law <jamie@proskow.nita>
DATE:	December 29, YR-3
SUBJECT:	Closing: Sportslifeware Acquisition

Jamie,

Per our earlier telephone conversation, I have had a chance to personally go over the closing packet. I know your client has been concerned. But I can confirm that the Asset Purchase Agreement, the Financial Statement, and the other closing documents are fine and all set for the closing tomorrow. I anticipate that the closing will be smooth and quick. Thanks for your patience in this matter. I am having the packet sent over to you by courier so you have a chance to look at it before we get together tomorrow. It has been a pleasure working with you. I look forward to seeing you tomorrow.

Motions and Materials for Program

ONE: MOTION TO DISMISS

I. EXERCISE

Defendant Sam Hanson has filed a motion to dismiss Claim II of Paul's complaint against him for failure to state a cause upon which relief can be granted under Rules 12(b)(6) and 9(b) of the Federal Rules of Civil Procedure. Alternatively, Hanson has also moved for a more definite statement pursuant to Rule 12(e).

B's for the Defendant Sam Hanson

Prepare to argue that the fraud in the inducement claim against Hanson for alleged fraudulent concealment should be dismissed. You may also argue for a more definite statement.

A's for the Plaintiff Michelle Paul

Prepare to argue in opposition to the motion to dismiss the complaint and the motion for a more definite statement. In preparing arguments, both sides may rely on and use (i) the attached Memorandum of Law and accompanying case and (ii) the complaint.

Assume for purposes of this assignment that no answer has been filed. In making your arguments, you may refer to only those facts contained in the complaint and the documents attached to the complaint. Remember that this is a Rule 12 motion, NOT a Rule 56 motion for summary judgment.

You should not read all the cases cited in the Memorandum of Law. You should only read the FDIC case attached to this motion. It may be helpful to read that case before reading the Memorandum of Law. Possible arguments for each side have been included in the memorandum. Although you should not do any independent legal research, you are not required to use nor are you limited by these arguments.

II. Memorandum of Law

TO: FILE

FROM: ASSOCIATE

RE: RULE 12(b)(6) MOTION TO DISMISS

A.   Factual Background

Paul alleges fraud in the inducement against Hanson, alleging that Hanson intentionally concealed from Paul information he had a duty to disclose to her. Her allegations surround Hanson's role in the sale of her business, Sportslifeware, to Dynamo and its owner, Arthur Dillon. Hanson had represented Dillon and Dynamo in past matters and again represented these defendants for this transaction. His representation began immediately after a memorandum of understanding was reached between Dillon and Paul, in March of YR-3, and continued to the closing of the deal in December of YR-3. The memorandum of understanding between Paul and Dillon provided that Dillon would pay Paul a total of $6 million for Sportslifeware, with a $500,000 down payment before closing and a $5.5 million payment in September of YR-2. As a condition of the agreement, Dillon was to provide financial statements to Paul, both at the signing of the memorandum of understanding and at the time of the closing, certifying that he was worth a minimum of $13 million. The financial statements are attached to the complaint. Both financial statements show identical assets and liabilities and indicate that Dillon was worth over $13 million. The financial statements were prepared by Dillon, signed by him, and purported to accurately reflect his assets and liabilities. Hanson delivered the financial statement prepared before closing to Paul's attorney. Hanson did not sign either of the financial statements.

Paul alleges in her complaint that while serving as Dillon and Dynamo's attorney, Hanson concealed information from her about Dillon's finances in order to induce her to complete the sale. Hanson told Paul and her attorney that he was intimately aware of Dynamo and Dillon's finances. In July YR-3, before closing, when Paul's attorney told Hanson that Paul was having second thoughts about the sale and willing to walk away from it, Hanson said he would personally review and handle all closing documents to make sure they were fine. Again immediately before closing, Hanson represented to Paul's attorney that he reviewed all the closing documents and the financial statement of Dec YR-3, and they were "fine." Paul claims that Hanson knew at the time of the representations that Dillon's net worth was less than $13 million, knew the entries on the financial statement were not accurate, and yet falsely told her attorney that the financial statement was "fine," thereby fraudulently concealing Dillon's true financial condition. As a result, she claims that she is damaged in the amount of $6 million.

B.   Law

1. Rule 12(b)(6)

Rule 12(b)(6) of the Federal Rules of Civil Procedure authorizes a district court to dismiss a claim on the basis of a "failure to state a claim upon which relief can be granted." Fed. R. Civ. P. 12(b)(6). When ruling upon a motion to dismiss under Rule 12(b)(6), it is the court's responsibility to accept as true the complaint's factual allegations and draw all inferences in the plaintiff's favor. *DeMuria v. Hawkes*, 328

F.3d 704, 706 (2d Cir. 2003). According to the U.S. Supreme Court:

> To survive a motion to dismiss, a complaint must contain sufficient fac-
> tual matter, accepted as true, "to state a claim to relief that is plausible on
> its face." A claim has facial plausibility when the plaintiff pleads factual
> content that allows the court to draw the reasonable inference that the
> defendant is liable for the misconduct alleged. The plausibility standard
> is not akin to a "probability requirement," but it asks for more than a
> sheer possibility that a defendant has acted unlawfully. Where a com-
> plaint pleads facts that are 'merely consistent with' a defendant's liability,
> it "stops short of the line between possibility and plausibility of 'entitle-
> ment to relief." *Ashcroft v. Iqbal*, 556 U.S. 662, 678 (2009) [quotations
> omitted].

2.   Rule 8(a)—Short and Plain Statement

In order for a district court to consider a Rule 12(b)(6), it must interpret Rule 8(a)'s requirement that a complaint contain a "short and plain statement of the claim," showing that the claimant is entitled to re-lief. Fed. R. Civ. P. 8(a). A complaint must contain "more than an unadorned, the defendant-unlawfully-harmed-me accusation." *Id.* Despite the liberal pleading standard of Rule 8, to survive a motion to dismiss, a complaint must allege "a plausible entitlement to relief." *Bell Atl. Corp. v. Twombly*, 550 U.S. 544 (2007).

3.   Rule 9(b)—Pleading Special Matters

Rule 8(a), however, must harmonize with Rule 9(b), which requires that all claims of fraud or mistake be pled with particularity. Fed. R. Civ. P. 9(b). To satisfy the particularity requirement, the complaint must sufficiently specify the time, place, and content of the false representations or omissions, as well as the identity of the person who made the misrepresentations or failed to make complete disclosure. *See McCauley v. Home Loan Inv. Bank, F.S.B.*, 710 F.3d 551, 559 (4th Cir. 2013).

On the other hand, Rule 9(b) permits malice, intent, knowledge, or other condition of mind of a person to be averred generally. Although the scienter requirement for a claim of fraud need not be plead with particularity, plaintiffs are required to allege facts that give rise to a strong inference of fraudulent intent in order to avoid abuse; the requisite "strong inference" of fraud may be established either by alleging facts to show that defendants had both the motive and opportunity to commit fraud, or by alleging facts that constitute strong circumstantial evidence of conscious misbehavior or recklessness. *Kuklachev v. Gelfman*, 600 F. Supp. 2d 437 (E.D.N.Y. 2009). "Where motive is not apparent, it is still possible to plead scienter by identifying circumstances indicating conscious behavior by the defendant, though the strength of the circumstantial allegations must be correspondingly greater." *Beck v. Mfrs. Hanover Trust Co.*, 820 F.2d 46, 50 (2d Cir. 1987), *overruled on other grounds by United States v. Indelicato*, 865 F.2d 1370 (2d Cir. 1989) (en banc). This is a highly fact-based inquiry.

> To survive dismissal under the "conscious misbehavior" theory, the plain-
> tiffs must show that they alleged reckless conduct by the defendant, which
> is at the least, conduct which is highly unreasonable and which represents

an extreme departure from the standards of ordinary care to the extent that the danger was either known to the defendant or so obvious that the defendant must have been aware of it." *Honeyman v. Hoyt (In Re Carter-Wallace, Inc. Secs. Litig.*, 220 F.3d 36, 39 (2d Cir. 2000).

The requirements of Rule 9(b) are "vigorously enforced" where allegations of fraud by omission are made against professionals, such as attorneys. *FDIC v. U.S. Mortgage Corp.*, 132 F. Supp. 3d 369 (E.D. N.Y. 2015). This protects the reputation and goodwill of a defendant from harm by unfounded allegations of fraud. *Id.* at 387.

4. Fraud

Fraudulent inducement by concealment is a state common law cause of action. Under Nita law, fraudulent concealment may be pled by alleging that the defendant had a duty to disclose material information to the plaintiff and breached that duty by intentionally concealing or omitting the material information, which resulted in harm to the plaintiff. *FDIC*, 132 F. Supp. 3d 369.

In paragraph number 24 of her complaint, Paul alleges that Hanson committed fraud in the inducement of this contract by concealing information from her about Dillon's financial condition.

5. Duty of Hanson to Disclose Financial Condition of Dillon

To prevail under a fraudulent concealment allegation, a plaintiff must demonstrate the existence of a duty running between the parties. As a general rule, an attorney has no duty to a non-client with whom she is not in privity. *Id* at 387. Liability of professionals to speak with care to third parties is imposed only where they have a special relationship with the third party that "approaches privity." *Id.* For example, if an attorney has issued an opinion letter to his client knowing that the purpose of the letter was reliance by a third party on its contents, then a special relationship is formed between the attorney and the third party. *Id.* This is so because under the circumstances 1) the attorney clearly holds herself out to be an expert in a particular area, 2) reliance on the opinion by the third party is the "end and aim" of the representation, and 3) therefore a special relationship exists justifying reliance on the lawyer's speech. *Id.* at 388.

6. Motion for a More Definite Statement under Rule 12(e)

If a pleading is "so vague or ambiguous" that the defendant cannot "reasonably be required to frame a response," the defendant may file a motion for a more definite statement under Rule 12(e) of the Federal Rules of Civil Procedure. The motion must "point out the defects complained of and the details desired." *Id.* To withstand a Rule 12(e) motion, the allegations must be sufficiently specific to provide adequate notice to the defendant. *Bell Atlantic Corp. v. Twombly*, 550 U.S. 544, 590 (2007). If the court orders a more definite statement and the order is not complied with in 14 days, the court may strike the pleading or issue any appropriate order. Fed. R. Civ. P. 12(e).

III. Possible Arguments for Hanson

Under Rule 9(b), a complaint of fraud must be pled with particularity and must allege facts sufficient to support a strong inference there was a duty to disclose and fraudulent intent. Even as Rule 9(b) provides a heightened standard for pleading fraud, a still higher standard must be reached in a claim of fraud against an attorney. *FDIC*, 132 F. Supp. 3d at 387. This difficult hurdle is designed to protect the reputation and goodwill of an attorney against unfounded allegations of fraud. *Id.* Plaintiff did not allege adequate facts to support either a duty to disclose or fraudulent intent.

Paul alleges that Hanson had a duty to disclose his knowledge that the personal financial statement submitted at closing was not accurate. A plaintiff pursuing this theory must allege the facts that give rise to a duty to disclose with the specificity required by Rule 9(b). The pleadings do not support such a duty between non-client Paul and attorney Hanson. Courts have recognized a relationship approaching privity with a third party when the attorney issued an opinion letter to his client in connection with a transaction for the purpose of reliance by the third party on its contents. *FDIC* at 387–388. In those circumstances, the lawyer holds himself out as an expert in a particular area and reliance on the opinion letter is the "end and the aim" of the lawyer's engagement. Here, the complaint does not allege that the purpose or "end and aim" of Hanson's engagement by Dillon was reliance by Paul on any opinion letter. In fact, Hanson had represented Dillon and Dynamo from the negotiation of the agreement to the closing. The "end and aim" of his representation was to represent Dillon's interest throughout the entirety of the transaction. Furthermore, Hanson issued no opinion letter or report. He did not sign the financial statements; he merely reviewed and delivered the financial statements and other closing documents to Paul's attorney, stating they were "fine." This statement does not equate to an opinion letter placing Hanson in privity with Paul.

Nor does the complaint set forth enough facts to support that Hanson fraudulently intended to conceal information from Paul. No facts are alleged that give rise to any motive for Hanson to fail to disclose information to Paul. The complaint does not allege that Hanson received any concrete or personal benefit from concealing information; he simply acted as Dillon's attorney. Without a showing of motive, Paul must plead facts showing conscious misbehavior on the part of Hanson. Conscious misbehavior requires alleging conduct that is completely unreasonable and is an extreme departure from standards of ordinary care to the extent that the danger was either known to Hanson or so obvious that he must have been aware of it. Because Hanson did not represent Paul and had no duty to disclose any information to her, any failure to disclose was not completely unreasonable or an extreme departure from standards of ordinary care.

Paul's factual allegations contained in her complaint must also state a claim that is plausible on its face. Her complaint does not. The facts alleged in the complaint do not plausibly allege a duty on the part of Hanson or any fraudulent intent of Hanson for the same reasons the complaint is not specific enough under Rule 9(b).

Furthermore, it is not plausible that Paul relied on Hanson's statements. The two financial statements were identical in every aspect but the dates, yet issued nine months apart. It was incumbent on Paul to look into the plausibility of Dillon, her buyer, having identical assets and liabilities over a nine-month period. If, as she alleges, the financial statement of Dillon was critical to the sale, a cursory review of the documents would signal that the financial statements were inaccurate, at least suspicious, and prompt her to inquire further.

IV. POSSIBLE ARGUMENTS FOR PAUL

Rule 12(b)(6) requires the court to accept as true the complaint's factual allegations and accept as true all inferences in the plaintiff's favor. Here, plaintiff states claims that are factual and plausible on their face, and meet the heightened requirements for pleading fraud particularity. At issue here is Paul's claim of fraudulent inducement, which is satisfied by Hanson's failure to disclose Dillon's financial condition.

Paul sold her company to Dillon with the specific proviso that he give her a personal guarantee, backed by a financial statement establishing a personal net worth of at least $13 million at the time of the closing. The complaint alleges that she only agreed to a down payment of $500,000 on a $6 million deal only upon Dillon's assurances that he was worth at least $13 million. Accurate financial statements were essential terms of the agreement.

Hanson represented Dillon at the time the memorandum of understanding was signed, and he knew that it was important for the financial statements to accurately reflect Dillon's finances. Hanson knew that the delays in closing had affected Paul's confidence in Dillon's financial worthiness to the point that Paul contemplated pulling out of the agreement. Hanson gave specific assurances to Paul's attorney that he, Hanson, was intimately aware of the finances of Dillon and Dynamo. Hanson knew that, to be accurate, the financial statement of December 23, YR-3, must have reflected Dillon's actual assets and net worth on that date. Hanson knew that Dillon was having financial hardships and was worth less than $13 million. Despite this knowledge, on the day before closing, Hanson represented in an email to Paul's attorney that he had personally reviewed the closing documents, including the personal financial statement, and they were "fine." Hanson never disclosed to Paul that Dillon was having financial difficulties.

Because of Hanson's knowledge of the terms of the deal, knowledge of Dillon's finances, and knowledge of the importance that Paul placed on an accurate financial statement, these facts and all reasonable inferences therefrom are sufficient to establish that Hanson intended to fraudulently conceal Dillon's and Dynamo's financial problems in order to induce Paul to sell her business. Plausibility does not require probability as this proceeding is in its infancy—before even an answer has been filed, let alone discovery commenced.

Additionally, the facts of the complaint plausibly and sufficiently allege that Hanson owed a duty of disclosure to Paul. Although Paul was a non-client, Hanson's representations were analogous to the kind of expert advice provided in an opinion letter. As stated in the *FDIC* decision, the issuance of an opinion letter to a third party can give rise to privity when the lawyer holds himself out to be an expert in a particular area and reliance on the opinion by the third party is the "end and aim" of the engagement by the lawyer. Hanson represented that he was intimately familiar with Dillon's finances. When Paul had second thoughts about going through with the sale, Hanson promised her attorney that he would personally review all closing documents. He later assured Paul's attorney that he had personally reviewed the closing packet, and he confirmed that the financial statement was fine. Hanson rendered an opinion on the soundness of the finances of his client. Although Hanson's opinion was not transmitted in a letter but rather in an email, the distinction is meaningless. By relating this opinion, Hanson failed to disclose that his client was now worth less than $13 million and that the financial statement submitted for closing was not accurate. The complaint sufficiently alleges that this opinion email was issued to induce Paul to complete the sale. The allegations sufficiently aver that Hanson held himself out as an expert in Dillon's finances and that Hanson intended Paul to rely on his assurances so that she would go through with the sale. This is enough to satisfy the requirement of Nita law that the "end and aim" of Hanson's engagement was encouraging Paul to rely on Hanson's false statements.

As to Hanson's argument that Paul's reliance on Hanson's statements is implausible, because the two financial statements were identical, the information about Dillon and Dynamo's finances was not available to Paul. Hanson knew that Paul was completely dependent upon Dillon to accurately represent his financial condition.

V. CASE LAW

FDIC v. Ezraty
132 F.Supp. 3d 369
United States District Court,
E.D. New York.

Signed Sept. 15, 2015

Spatt, District Judge

Presently before the Court is a motion by the Cross-Defendant Ira S. Ezratty to dismiss the claims that are asserted against him contained in the second amended third-party complaint of the Defendant/Cross-Complainant U.S. Mortgage Corporation.

* * *

On January 29, 2013, the Plaintiff Federal Deposit Insurance Corporation ("FDIC"), in its capacity as the Receiver of AmTrust Bank of Cleveland, Ohio ("AmTrust"), commenced this action against U.S. Mortgage Corporation d/b/a U.S. Mortgage Concepts ("USMC"). The complaint in that action (the "Main Complaint") principally alleged that USMC, a mortgage broker, breached the terms of a Master Broker Agreement.

* * *

The basis for the alleged breach originates not with USMC, but with the individual Cross–Defendants, namely, Lawrence Conde ("Lawrence"), Michael J. Conde ("Michael"), and Marian T. Campi a/k/a Marian Conde ("Marian", together with Lawrence and Michael, the "Condes"). It is alleged that these individuals engaged in a fraudulent scheme to obtain a home mortgage loan. In particular, the Condes allegedly provided false and misleading information to USMC in order to qualify for loan financing. USMC then allegedly supplied that same false information to AmTrust. Allegedly, AmTrust relied on this information and approved a $1.5 Million loan for the Condes, to its detriment.

It is alleged in the Main Complaint that USMC's act of supplying the false and misleading information to AmTrust constituted a breach of their Master Broker Agreement. Thus, in Receivership, the FDIC sought to recoup those losses from USMC on AmTrust's behalf.

* * *

Relevant here, the second amended third-party complaint alleges that Ezratty is an attorney who is licensed to practice law in New York State and maintains an office in Mineola, New York. Further, the second amended third party complaint alleges that Lawrence retained Ezratty in connection with the loan transaction outlined above. In this regard, Ezratty allegedly had knowledge of the Condes's scheme and reviewed, counseled, and supervised Lawrence in his execution of numerous documents related to obtaining the loan, all of which are alleged to have contained materially false and misleading information.

* * *

Michael and Marian are married. At all relevant times, they owned a residential home located at 12 Crooked Oak Road in Port Jefferson, New York (the "Premises").

Allegedly, Michael and Marian filed for bankruptcy.

In order to avoid losing the Premises in bankruptcy, Michael and Marian allegedly devised a scheme that would create the appearance of a legitimate sale of the Premises. In this regard, they arranged to "sell" the Premises to Michael's father, Lawrence. This would allegedly permit Michael and Marian to continue residing at the Premises and, ultimately, to repurchase it from Lawrence.

In furtherance of this Scheme, Lawrence allegedly sought to obtain a home mortgage loan from USMC. It is alleged that Lawrence intended to use the loan proceeds to purchase the Premises. Is it further alleged that Lawrence intended to secure a loan in an amount greater than would be necessary to purchase the Premises, so that Michael and Marian could use the surplus loan proceeds to settle with the bankruptcy trustee and obtain a global release of their bankruptcy debts.

According to the Main Complaint, the Condes collectively endeavored to hide their Scheme from USMC. In this regard, Lawrence, posing as a bone fide purchaser, allegedly informed USMC that he desired to purchase the residency from one "Marian Campi." Campi is Marian's maiden name, and, allegedly, was used deliberately in order to conceal the true nature of the transaction from USMC, namely, an intrafamilial sale.

* * *

Central to USMC's claims against Ezratty is the following allegation.

> [P]rior to March 2006, Lawrence, and/or Michael and Marian, and/or Christensen provided Ezratty with a copy of the Stipulation and/or informed Ezratty of the sum and substance of the Stipulation and Scheme, including the following: (i) that Lawrence and Michael and Marian were related; (ii) that Lawrence was purchasing the Premises pursuant to the Stipulation and solely for the purpose of facilitating Michael's and Marian's extraction of equity from the Premises and remov[ing] the impending threat of losing the Premises through the Bankruptcy Case; (iii) that Lawrence did not intend to occupy the Premises; (iv) that Michael and Marian intended to remain living in the Premises even after the purchase/sale transaction was consummated; (v) that Lawrence did not intend on

assuming any financial responsibility for the Premises, including payments on any loan secured by the Premises, property taxes, maintenance,
or repairs, but that Michael and Marian would continue to be responsible
for those obligations; and (vi) within a year or so, Lawrence would deed
the Premises back to Michael and Marian.

It is Ezratty's alleged knowledge of these important facts that supports many, if not all, of USMC's claims
against him.

Further, the complaint alleges that Ezratty, with the specific knowledge outlined above, reviewed, counseled, and/or supervised Lawrence in preparing multiple fraudulent documents that were relied upon
by USMC and AmTrust in approving the Loan, including a Uniform Residential Loan Application
(the "Application"). It is alleged that the Application, which was used to apply for financing to purchase
the Premises, falsely indicated that Lawrence intended to occupy the Premises as his primary residence.
USMC asserts that, without such a representation, Lawrence would not have been eligible for financing
or would have been offered less favorable financing terms. Allegedly, Lawrence also supplied a "Disclosure
Notice" in which he reiterated his intention to occupy the Premises within 30 days of closing.

In addition, Lawrence allegedly supplied a document entitled "Borrower's Certification & Authorization," which certified that the information contained in the Application and related documents was true
and complete; contained no misrepresentations; and did not omit any pertinent information.

* * *

Under Fed. R. Civ. P. 8(a)(2), a pleading that states a claim for relief must contain "a short and plain
statement of the claim showing that the pleader is entitled to relief." The pleading standard announced
in Rule 8 "does not require 'detailed factual allegations,' but it demands more than an unadorned, the-
defendant-unlawfully-harmed-me accusation." *Ashcroft v. Iqbal*, 556 U.S. 662, 677–78 (2009) (quoting
Bell Atl. Corp. v. Twombly, 550 U.S. 544, (2007)). "A pleading that offers 'labels and conclusions' or 'a
formulaic recitation of the elements of a cause of action will not do.'"

Rather, to survive a motion to dismiss under Rule 12(b)(6), "a complaint must contain sufficient factual
matter, accepted as true, to '"state claim for relief that is plausible on its face."' and the "[f]actual allegations must be enough to raise a right to relief above the speculative level." *Twombly*, 550 U.S. at 557.

Furthermore, claims based on fraud are subject to the heightened pleading standard found in
Fed. R. Civ. P. 9(b). In particular, a party asserting fraud "must state with particularity the circumstances
constituting fraud or mistake." Fed. R. Civ. P. 9(b). "Rule 9(b) is satisfied when the complaint specifies
'the time, place, speaker, and content of the alleged misrepresentations;' how the misrepresentations
were fraudulent; and the details that 'give rise to a strong inference that the defendant[ ] had an intent to
defraud, knowledge of the falsity, or a reckless disregard for the truth.'" *Schwartzco Enters. LLC v. TMH
Mgmt., LLC*, 60 F. Supp. 3d 331.

* * *

A claim based on fraud may also be pled by alleging that the defendant owed a duty of disclosure to the plaintiff, and breached that duty by intentionally concealing or omitting relevant information, which resulted in harm to the plaintiff.

A duty of disclosure generally arises in three circumstances: (i) the parties are in a fiduciary or confidential relationship; (ii) one party makes a partial or ambiguous statement that requires additional disclosure to avoid misleading the other party; and (iii) one party possesses superior knowledge, not readily available to the other, and knows that the other is acting on the basis of mistaken knowledge. (citations omitted).

A plaintiff pursuing this theory "'must allege [the] facts giving rise to a duty to disclose' with the specificity required by Rule 9(b)." (citations omitted). *See Merrill Lynch, Pierce, Fenner & Smith v. Young,* 91-cv-2923, 1994 U.S. Dist. LEXIS 2929, at *33-*34 (S.D.N.Y. Mar. 15, 1994) (stating that plaintiff must plead with "particularity" the "context in which a duty to disclose may have arisen," and "[i]nferences and allusions" to circumstances under which "a general duty to disclose may arise do not withstand 9(b) scrutiny").

In this regard, the Second Circuit has "vigorously enforced Rule 9(b)" where, as here, allegations of fraud by omission are made against professionals, such as attorneys. (citations omitted).

* * *

USMC contends that: (i) Ezratty possessed superior knowledge of the underlying transaction; (ii) which was not readily available to USMC; and (iii) he knew that USMC was acting on the basis of mistaken knowledge in evaluating Lawrence's eligibility for a home mortgage loan.

At the outset, the Court takes special note of the fact that Ezratty is an attorney and, therefore, the standard to which USMC's allegations are held is necessarily higher than it might be with respect to a layperson. *See Quintel [v. Citibank],* 589 F. Supp. at 1243–44 (noting that the Second Circuit has "vigorously enforced Rule 9(b)" in cases involving fraud allegations against professionals); *DiVittorio [v. Equidyne Extractive Indus.,* 822 F.2d 1242 at 1247 (2d Cir. 1987)], (a pleading under Rule 9(b) must be sufficient, inter alia, to protect a defendant from harm to its reputation or goodwill by unfounded allegations of fraud).

In this case, it is not alleged that Ezratty represented USMC; that Ezratty owed a fiduciary duty to USMC; that Ezratty and USMC were in privity; or that they enjoyed some other special relationship that was so close as to approach privity. There also is no plausible allegation that Ezratty was a party to the underlying transaction or that he made any relevant statement or representation upon which USMC relied. On the contrary, USMC appears to allege only that Ezratty acted as Lawrence's agent in connection with his purchase of the Premises and was, therefore, under an obligation to disclose to third-party non-clients whatever relevant information he possessed. Moreover, USMC contends that his failure to do so exposes him to liability for fraud.

However, USMC cites to no controlling authority for the existence of such an expansive duty, and the Court's own research has revealed none. Actually, the prevailing law appears to dictate a far narrower approach—one that insulates attorneys from liability for all but the most overt actions which are designed specifically to induce third-parties' reliance. In the Court's view, the complaint does not state any facts by which it could be considered plausible that Ezratty owed such a duty to USMC.

In reaching this conclusion, the Court is persuaded by the rule enunciated in *Doehla v. Wathne Ltd.*, where the court noted that a lawyer "may owe a duty of care to his clients by virtue of a special relationship of confidence and trust that arises from his training and expertise," but that, as a "general rule," a lawyer "does not owe a fiduciary duty to non-clients with whom he is not in privity." *Doehla*, 1999 U.S. Dist. LEXIS 11787, at *57 (S.D.N.Y. Aug. 3, 1999) In fact, in the absence of a fiduciary relationship, "New York courts have imposed liability on professionals for their failure to speak with care to third-parties . . . only where they have a special relationship with the third-party that 'approaches that of privity.'" *Id.* at *19. In this regard, the court in *Doehla* noted:

> [T]he only cases of which this Court is aware holding that an attorney had, or was properly alleged to have had, a relationship approaching privity with a third-party are those in which the attorney issued an 'opinion letter' to his client in connection with a transaction for the purpose of reliance by the third-party on its contents. Such cases meet the standard established under New York law because the lawyer clearly holds himself out to be an expert in a particular area, reliance on the opinion by the third-party is the "end and aim" of the engagement of the lawyer, and therefore a special relationship exists justifying reliance on the lawyer's speech. (citations omitted).

Thus, in *Doehla*, the court found that no duty of disclosure existed because, as here, (i) the attorney in question had not represented the plaintiff, and (ii) there was no special relationship between the attorney and the plaintiff which approached privity. In addition, the court noted that the complaint had failed to allege that the purpose or "end and aim" of the lawyer's engagement was to induce reliance by the plaintiff on allegedly negligently furnished declarations. In particular, the attorney in *Doehla* had "issued no opinion letter or report upon which [the plaintiff] was urged to rely" and "[e]ven if he had, there [wa]s nothing to suggest that [the lawyer] held himself out as having expertise on the particular subject involved."

Applying these principles, the Court finds that the second amended third-party complaint fails to state facts which are sufficient to create a duty running from Ezratty to USMC. In particular, in this case, as in *Doehla*, there appears to be no dispute that Ezratty did not represent USMC; did not hold himself out as an expert on any relevant subject matter; and did not render an opinion or written report upon which he intended USMC to rely. Further, in the Court's view, it is implausible to conclude that the "end and aim" of Ezratty's engagement was to induce USMC's reliance on fraudulent declarations. On the contrary, as noted above, there is no plausible allegation that Ezratty even made a statement or representation regarding the underlying transaction. It has been recognized under similar circumstances that such nondisclosure, without more, cannot form the basis for a fraud claim. (citations omitted).

Based on the foregoing, the Court finds that USMC failed to state enough specific facts regarding the "context in which [Ezratty's] duty to disclose may have arisen," to satisfy Rule 9(b). Accordingly, to the extent Ezratty seeks to dismiss the Twenty-Ninth Cause of Action on the grounds that he did not have a duty of disclosure to USMC, his motion is granted.

TWO: Motion to Compel Discovery— Crime-Fraud Exception

I. Exercise

Pursuant to the court's order for expedited discovery for purposes of the preliminary injunction hearing, the parties have exchanged requests for production of documents, filed interrogatories, and noticed depositions. Discovery is still in the early stages. In response to Plaintiff Michelle Paul's discovery request, Defendants Dillon and Dynamo Sporting Goods have produced a privilege log listing eight withheld documents based on attorney-client privilege. For purposes of this motion, assume that Defendant Hanson has been dismissed.

Michelle Paul has moved, under Fed. R. Civ. P. 37(a)(3), to compel production of these documents. She asserts there is a reasonable basis to believe an in camera review may reveal evidence that the crime-fraud exception to the attorney client privilege applies, making the documents subject to discovery under Fed. R. Civ. P. 26. Defendants oppose the motion and have filed a motion for a protective order for these documents. Paul's counsel will argue the motions first.

A's for the Plaintiff Michelle Paul

Identify the documents on defendants' privilege log for which you are seeking an in camera review, and prepare to argue in support of your motion to compel production and in opposition to the motion for a protective order on the basis of the crime-fraud exception to the attorney client privilege.

B's for the Defendant Arthur Dillon, Sam Hanson and Dynamo Sporting Goods

Prepare to argue in opposition to the plaintiff's motion to compel production of certain documents and in support of your motion for protective order on the basis of the crime-fraud exception to the attorney client privilege.

In preparing arguments, both sides may rely on and use (i) the privilege log, (ii) the attached list of exhibits in support of Michelle Paul's motion to compel, and the (iii) Memorandum of Law and accompanying cases. Possible arguments for each side are included in the memorandum. You are not required to use these arguments nor are you limited to these arguments.

> **Please do not conduct additional legal research. You should read the attached "key cases" and may rely on the cases cited in the memorandum of law. However, do not read any of the cases cited in those materials. Also, during argument, you may not argue other cases that you may know about. In other words, your universe of law is contained in the materials that follow.**

II. Memorandum of Law

TO: FILE
FROM: ASSOCIATE
RE: MOTION TO COMPEL AND FOR PROTECTIVE ORDER

A. Factual Background

As part of Paul's fraudulent inducement claim in her complaint, Paul alleges that under the terms of the Memorandum of Agreement, executed on March 24, YR-3, Dillon agreed to purchase Sportslifeware for a total purchase price of $6 million. Dillon agreed to a cash payment of $500,000 at closing and to pay the remaining portion of the purchase price, $5.5 million, no later than September 1, YR-2. To persuade Paul to accept the deferred payment, Dillon agreed to personally guarantee the payment of the purchase price. To do so, Dillon provided a personal financial statement showing he had a financial net worth of $15 million. Dillon agreed to provide an updated personal financial statement at closing. Paul had the right to terminate the agreement to sell if Dillon's net worth, as shown on his financial statement at closing, was less than $13 million.

During negotiations, Dillon told Paul that his lawyer, Sam Hanson, represented Dillon in all his business and financial dealings and knew his business and finances better than anyone. Hanson and Paul's attorney finalized the terms of the asset purchase agreement in summer YR-3, but Dillon postponed the closing until December 30. The day before closing, Hanson emailed Paul's attorney and said he had personally reviewed the closing documents because of the delay. He assured Paul's attorney that the financial statement enclosed with the documents was fine.

The financial statement submitted with the closing documents is identical to the one provided in March YR-3. Paul alleges that Dillon's net worth at the time of closing was less than $13 million. Paul claims that Dillon knew the statements were false and made them intentionally for the purpose of inducing Paul to sell her business. Paul also contends that Hanson knew the personal financial statement was not accurate and failed to disclose the information, while falsely telling her the statement was fine.

B. Law

1. Motions to Compel Discovery—Fed. R. Civ. P. 37(a)

Federal Rule of Civil Procedure 37(a) provides that "[a] party . . . may apply for an order compelling disclosure or discovery." This motion can be used to compel any discovery that is required to be produced pursuant to Rule 26. Fed. R. Civ. P. 37(a).

2. Motions for Protective Orders—Fed. R. Civ. P. 26(c)

Federal Rule of Civil Procedure 26(c) authorizes a party to seek an order "that certain matters not be inquired into, or that the scope of the disclosures or discovery be limited to certain matters." Fed. R. Civ. P. 26(c)(4).

3. The Attorney-Client Privilege

Federal courts have recognized a privilege for communications between attorney and client. *See Upjohn Co. v. United States*, 449 U.S. 383, 389 (1981). The privilege exists to "encourage full and frank communication between attorneys and their clients." *Id.* The privilege is designed so that the client may obtain "the aid of persons having knowledge of the law and skilled in its practice." *Hunt v. Blackburn*, 128 U.S. 464, 470 (1888).

4. The Crime-Fraud Exception to the Attorney-Client Privilege

a. The Nature of the Exception

The attorney-client privilege is the oldest confidential communications privilege known to the common law, and one that has been regarded as "worthy of maximum legal protection." *Haines v. Ligget Grp.*, 975 F.2d 81, 89 (3d Cir. 1992.) Notwithstanding its importance, the attorney-client privilege is not absolute. The United States Supreme Court has recognized the crime-fraud exception to the attorney-client privilege. *United States v. Zolin*, 491 U.S. 554, 556 (1989). Although the protection of open client and attorney communication is central to the proper functioning of our adversary system, the seal of secrecy between lawyer and client does not extend to communications "made for the purpose of getting advice for the commission of a fraud or crime." *Id.* at 563.

"Timing is critical. The client must have been 'engaged in or planning a criminal or fraudulent scheme when he sought the advice of counsel to further the scheme.'" *Triple Five of Minnesota, Inc. v. Simon et al.*, 213 F.R.D. 324, 326 (D. Minn. 2002.) "Moreover, the legal advice must have been obtained to further the fraudulent activity. *Id.* "[F]or advice to be used 'in furtherance' of a crime or fraud, the advice must advance, or the client must intend the advice to advance, the client's criminal or fraudulent purpose. The advice cannot merely relate to the crime or fraud." *In re Grand Jury Subpoena*, 745 F.3d 681, 693 (3d Cir. 2014).

The focus is on the client rather than on the attorney. For the crime-fraud exception to apply, all that is necessary is that the client misuse or intend to misuse the attorney's advice in furtherance of an improper purpose. The attorney does not have to be implicated in the crime or fraud or even have knowledge of the fraudulent scheme. *In re Grand Jury*, 705 F.3d 133, 157 (3d Cir. 2012). Because both the legal advice and the privilege are for the benefit of the client, it is the client's knowledge and intent that are relevant. *In re Napster, Inc. Copyright Litig.*, 479 F.3d 1078, 1090 (9th Cir. 2007).

b. The In Camera Review

The party wishing to assert the crime-fraud exception may request the court to engage in an in camera review of the disputed evidence to determine if the crime-fraud exception applies. *Zolin*, at 571–572. However, the court will not engage in "groundless fishing expeditions." *Id.* at 571. Therefore, the Supreme Court in *Zolin* set forth a two-step analysis in determining whether an in camera review is appropriate in a given case. First, a "threshold evidentiary showing" is required before a court may undertake an in camera review. Because in camera review "does not have the legal effect of terminating the privilege," and is thus a "smaller intrusion" on the attorney-client privilege than outright disclosure, "a lesser evidentiary showing is needed to trigger in camera review than necessary to ultimately overcome the privilege."

Id. at 572 (internal quotation marks omitted). The party seeking disclosure must make "'a showing of a factual basis adequate to support a good faith belief by a reasonable person' . . . that in camera review of the materials may reveal evidence to establish the claim that the crime-fraud exception applies." *Id.* at 572 (citations omitted).

The *Zolin* court stated this evidentiary showing necessary to trigger in camera review "need not be a stringent one." *Id.* at 572. The requesting party must make only a minimal showing that the crime-fraud exception could apply, and some speculation is required under the *Zolin* threshold. *In re Grand Jury Investigation*, 974 F.2d 1068, 1073 (9th Cir. 1992). Additionally, the threshold showing to obtain in camera review "may be met by using any relevant evidence, lawfully obtained, that has not been adjudicated to be privileged." *Zolin*, at p. 575.

Once the threshold showing has been made by the party seeking disclosure, the court moves to the second step in determining the propriety of an in camera review. The court must exercise its discretion whether to conduct such a review. *Zolin*, at 572. "The court should make the decision, in light of the facts and circumstances of the particular case, including, among other things, the volume of materials the court has been asked to review, the relative importance to the case of the alleged privileged information, and the likelihood that the evidence produced through in camera review, together with other available evidence then before the court, will establish that the crime-fraud exception does apply." *Id.*

Additionally, *Zolin* states that the court "is also free to defer its in camera review if it concludes that additional evidence in support of the crime-fraud exception may be available that is not allegedly privileged, and that production of the additional evidence will not unduly disrupt or delay the proceedings." *Id.* at 572.

c. Prima Facie Showing That Crime-fraud Exception Applies

Once the court has determined that a reasonable person could believe in good faith that an in camera review may reveal evidence establishing the application of the crime-fraud exception, the party seeking disclosure must make a prima facie showing that the crime fraud exception applies to the communications sought. The court may consider the content of the privileged documents in making the ultimate showing that the crime fraud exception applies and that the privilege should be overcome. See *Zolin*, at 568–70.

The phrase "prima facie" was used by the Supreme Court in *Clark v. United States*, 28 U.S. 1, 15 (1933) "to describe the showing needed to defeat the privilege. . . ." *Zolin*, at 563, fn. 7. But neither *Clark* nor *Zolin* clarified the necessary evidentiary showing for a prima facie case. The Supreme Court in *Zolin*, however, concluded that a greater evidentiary showing is required to overcome the privilege than is required to trigger in camera review. *Zolin*, at 572.

Courts of appeal are divided on the prima facie standard and have articulated the required measure of proof in different ways. The jurisdiction of Nita has adopted the "reasonable basis" standard, as used by Third and First Circuits. "A party seeking to apply the crime-fraud exception must demonstrate that there is a reasonable basis to suspect (1) that the privilege holder was committing or intending to commit a crime or fraud, and (2) that the attorney-client communication . . . was used in furtherance of that alleged crime or fraud." *(In re Grand Jury*, 705 F.3d 133, 155 (3d Cir. 2012).) "For advice to be used 'in furtherance' of a crime or fraud, the advice must advance, or the client must intend the advice to advance, the client's criminal or fraudulent purpose. The advice cannot merely relate to the crime or fraud." *In re Grand Jury Subpoena*, 745 F.3d 681, 693 (3d Cir. 2014). The Third Circuit has said the "reasonable basis" "is closest to the Supreme Court's pronouncement that, for the crime-fraud exception to apply, 'there must be something to give color to the charge' that the attorney-client communication was used in furtherance of a crime or fraud." *In re Grand Jury*, 705 F.3d at 153.

The prima facie standard is intended to be "reasonably demanding;" speculation is not sufficient. *Id.* at 153. As stated by the Ninth Circuit, applying a similar "reasonable cause" prima facie standard:

> [I]t isn't enough for the [party seeking disclosure] merely to allege that it has sneaking suspicion the client was engaging or intending to engage in a crime or fraud when it consulted the attorney. A threshold that low could discourage many would-be clients from consulting an attorney about entirely legitimate legal dilemmas. Rather, the district court must find "reasonable cause to believe" that the attorney's services were "utilized . . . in furtherance of the ongoing unlawful scheme." *In re Grand Jury Proceedings*, 87 F.3d 377, 381 (9th Cir.1996) (quoting *In re Grand Jury Proceedings*, 867 F.2d 539, 541).

Although "there must be 'prima facie evidence that [the application of the exception] has some foundation in fact,'" *Id.* at 151–152, quoting *Clark v. United States*, 289 U.S. 1, 15, "[a]t the same time, the party opposing the privilege is not required to introduce evidence sufficient to support a verdict of crime or fraud or even to show that it is more likely than not that the crime or fraud occurred." *In re Grand Jury*, 705 F.3d at 153–154.

III. Index of Exhibits to Plaintiff's Motion to Compel

A. Privilege Log Prepared on Behalf of Arthur Dillon, Sam Hanson, and Dynamo Sporting Goods

B. Declaration of Michelle Paul

C. Arthur Dillon's Personal Financial Statement, dated March 23, YR-3

D. Arthur Dillon's Personal Financial Statement, dated December 23, YR-3

E. Email from Sam Hanson to Jamie Norris, dated December 29, YR-3

Exhibit A

Privilege Log

Prepared on Behalf of Arthur Dillon, Sam Hanson, and Dynamo Sporting Goods

Date	Author	Recipient	Document Type	Subject Matter
3/24/YR-3	Dillon	Hanson	Letter/Fax	Acquisition of Sportslifeware
6/12/YR-3	Hanson	Dillon	Letter	Negotiations re: asset purchase agreement; selection of closing date
7/22/YR-3	Hanson	Dillon	Letter	Dillon mortgage; update re: Dynamo financing and selection of closing date
9/20/YR-3	Dillon	Hanson	Letter	Payment for legal services May through June; Dynamo payment due at closing
11/10/YR-3	Dillon	Hanson	Letter	Payment for legal services July through August; capital sources
12/26/YR-3	Dillon	Hanson	Letter	Acquisition closing and personal financial statement
12/28/YR-3	Hanson	Dillon	Email	Receipt of personal financial statement; readiness of acquisition closing documents
12/28/YR-3	Dillon	Hanson	Email	Approval of personal financial statement

Exhibit B

IN THE UNITED STATES DISTRICT COURT
FOR THE DISTRICT OF NITA

MICHELLE PAUL,)
Plaintiff)
)
v.) CIVIL ACTION NO. YR-1-1234
)
ARTHUR DILLON, et al.)
Defendants)

DECLARATION OF MICHELLE PAUL

Michelle Paul, under 28 U.S.C. § 1746, states the following:

1. I am the former owner of Sportslifeware, a company that manufactured and sold sportswear for women.

2. On March 24, YR-3, I met with Arthur Dillon to negotiate the sale of Sportslifeware to Dillon and his company, Dynamo Sporting Goods. Dillon and I agreed on terms that were memorialized in a Memorandum of Agreement that we signed the same day. The terms included:

(a) I agreed to sell my interest in Sportslifeware to Dillon and Dynamo for $6 million.

(b) Dillon and Dynamo agreed to pay $500,000 at closing and the remaining $5.5 million, plus interest, by September 1, YR-2

(c) The closing would be on a date selected by Dillon and Dynamo, but no later than December 31, YR-3.

(d) Dillon agreed to personally guarantee payment of the purchase price.

(e) To demonstrate his ability to fulfill his guaranty, Dillon provided a current Personal Financial Statement on March 24, YR-3, and agreed to provide at closing an updated Personal Financial Statement, current and accurate at that time.

(f) I would have the right to terminate the agreement to sell Sportslifeware if Dillon's net worth at closing, as shown on his Personal Financial Statement, was less than $13 million.

(g) Dillon's lawyer would be responsible for preparing the closing documents.

3. During the negotiation, Dillon told me that his lawyer, Sam Hanson, had represented him in all his business and financial dealings for years, and could finalize the deal faster than anyone else because, "he knows my business and finances better than anyone."

4. Originally, Dillon told me that he wanted to have the closing as soon as the closing documents could be finalized. The lawyers finalized the terms of the asset purchase agreement in July YR-3, but Dillon delayed closing until nearly the last possible date, December 30, YR-3.

5. I declare under penalty of perjury that the foregoing is true and correct. Executed on _____, YR-1.

Michelle Paul
_____
Michelle Paul

Exhibit C

Arthur Dillon's Personal Financial statement, dated March 23, YR-3

Personal Financial Statement Date of Statement: March 23, YR-3

Name (first, middle, last) Arthur R. Dillon	Birth date 4-1-YR-48	Phone number (212) 555-1212		Social security number 468-24-xxxx
Home address (include apt.) 540 8th Street	City, state, zip New York, NY 10004			How long? 20 years

If joint statement, list joint applicant financial information: N/A			Social security number of joint party:			

Assets S= single J = joint	Value	Liabilities	Loan Amount	Credit Limit	Monthly payment	Balance
Cash on hand, & unrestricted in banks **(Mo. market, checking, CDs)**	$ 825,000	Notes payable to banks	N/A			$ 825,000
Cash surrender value life insurance	$ 5,000,000	Loans against life ins.	($1,000,000)			$4,000,000
Retirement accounts (401K, IRA, etc.)		Loans against ret. accts.	N/A			
Listed (NYSE, AMEX) stocks, bonds		Margin loans				
		Credit cards	No balance carried			
Real estate (primary residence) **New York**	$ 2,000,000	Mortgage/rent (primary residence)	N/A			$2,000,000
Real estate (secondary residence) **Arizona**	$ 1,775,000	Mortgage (secondary residence)	N/A			$1,775,000
		Home equity loans	N/A			
Vehicles **Mercedes Benz, Lexus**	$ 100,000	Vehicle loans/ leases	N/A			$ 100,000
Notes/Accounts receivable		Taxes accrued but unpaid	N/A			
Other assets (describe) **Dynamo Sporting Goods—Owner**	$19,000,000	Other liabilities (describe) **Mortgage, inventory financing, equip. loans**	($12,700,000)		$ 14,568	$6,300,000
		Contingent Liabilities As guarantor or co-maker, Legal claims on leases or contracts	N/A			
TOTAL ASSETS	$28,700,000	**TOTAL LIABILITIES**	($13,700,000)	**NET WORTH** (assets minus liabilities)		$15 million

Income Information __Monthly_X_Annual Alimony, child support or separate maintenance income need not be listed.		Banking Relationships (Deposits only) Bank Name S=Single J=Joint				Cash Balance
Gross salary, wages, tips	$600,000	First National Bank of Nita				$825,000
Bonus/commissions (recurring)	350,000					
Other income (dividends, interest, etc.)	100,000					
TOTAL INCOME	$1,050,000	**TOTAL CASH**				$825,000

This financial statement is submitted as a separate attachment to my credit application. I warrant that there is no judgment against me nor lien unsatisfied upon my property except as shown, nor prior suit pending against me in any court, that no assets are pledged in any manner herein, and that this statement is true and complete and is offered for the purpose of obtaining and maintaining credit. With joint credit, all applicants must sign.

arthur Dillon   March 23, YR-3

Arthur Dillon's Personal Financial Statement, dated December 23, YR-3

Personal Financial Statement Date of Statement: December 23, YR-3

Name (first, middle, last) **Arthur R. Dillon**	Birth date **4-1-YR-48**	Phone number **(212) 555-1212**			Social security number **468-24-xxxx**	
Home address (include apt.) **540 8th Street**	City, state, zip **New York, NY 10004**				How long? **20 years**	
If joint statement, list joint applicant financial information: N/A				Social security number of joint party:		

Assets　　S= single 　　　　　J = joint	Value	Liabilities	Loan Amount	Credit Limit	Monthly payment	Balance
Cash on hand, & unrestricted in banks **(Mo. market, checking, CDs)**	$ 825,000	Notes payable to banks	N/A			$ 825,000
Cash surrender value life insurance	$ 5,000,000	Loans against life ins.	($1,000,000)			$4,000,000
Retirement accounts (401K, IRA, etc.)		Loans against ret. accts.	N/A			
Listed (NYSE, AMEX) stocks, bonds		Margin loans				
		Credit cards	No balance carried			
Real estate (primary residence) **New York**	$ 2,000,000	Mortgage/rent (primary residence)	N/A			$2,000,000
Real estate (secondary residence) **Arizona**	$ 1,775,000	Mortgage (secondary residence)	N/A			$1,775,000
		Home equity loans	N/A			
Vehicles **Mercedes Benz, Lexus**	$ 100,000	Vehicle loans/ leases	N/A			$ 100,000
Notes/Accounts receivable		Taxes accrued but unpaid	N/A			
Other assets (describe) **Dynamo Sporting Goods—Owner**	$19,000,000	Other liabilities (describe) **Mortgage, inventory financing, equip. loans**	($12,700,000)		$ 14,568	$6,300,000
		Contingent Liabilities As guarantor or co-maker, Legal claims on leases or contracts	N/A			
TOTAL ASSETS	**$28,700,000**	**TOTAL LIABILITIES**	**($13,700,000)**	NET WORTH (assets minus liabilities)		**$15 million**

Income Information __Monthly _X_ Annual Alimony, child support or separate maintenance income need not be listed.		Banking Relationships (Deposits only) Bank Name　　　　　　　　　S=Single 　　　　　　　　　　　　　　J=Joint		Cash Balance
Gross salary, wages, tips	$600,000	**First National Bank of Nita**		$825,000
Bonus/commissions (recurring)	350,000			
Other income (dividends, interest, etc.)	100,000			
TOTAL INCOME	**$1,050,000**	**TOTAL CASH**		**$825,000**

This financial statement is submitted as a separate attachment to my credit application. I warrant that there is no judgment against me nor lien unsatisfied upon my property except as shown, nor prior suit pending against me in any court, that no assets are pledged in any manner herein, and that this statement is true and complete and is offered for the purpose of obtaining and maintaining credit. With joint credit, all applicants must sign.

arthur Dillon　　　　　　　　　　　　12-23-YR-3

Jamie Norris

From:	samhanson@DHLlaw.nita
Sent:	December 29, YR-3
To:	Jamie Norris, Proskow & Proskow, Attorneys at Law <jamie@proskow.nita>
Subject:	Closing: Sportslifeware Acquisition

Jamie,

Per our earlier telephone conversation, I have had a chance to personally go over the closing packet. I know your client has been concerned. But I can confirm that the Asset Purchase Agreement, the Financial Statement, and the other closing documents are fine and all set for the closing tomorrow. I anticipate that the closing will be smooth and quick. Thanks for your patience in this matter. I am having the packet sent over to you so you have a chance to look at it before we get together tomorrow. It has been a pleasure working with you. I look forward to seeing you tomorrow.

IV. Possible Arguments for Paul

A. The Threshold Showing under *Zolin*

The threshold standard for the in camera review is not a high one. It requires only a minimal showing: the in camera review *may* reveal evidence to establish that the crime-fraud exception applies. "The judge should require a showing of a factual basis adequate to support a good faith basis by a reasonable person that in camera review of the materials may reveal evidence to establish the claim that the crime-fraud exception applies." *U.S. v. Zolin*, 491 U.S. 554 (1989). Here the showing has been made.

Sam Hanson was Dillon's attorney, who represented him in all business and financial matters. During the initial contract negotiations in March YR-3, Dillon told Paul that Hanson had handled all of his business and personal matters for years and knew Dillon's business and finances better than anyone. Thus, it is reasonable to believe that Dillon consulted with Hanson about any financial difficulties he faced between the March YR-3 Memorandum of Agreement and the December YR-3 closing.

Dillon initially stated he was eager to close the Sportslifeware deal as soon as possible after the Memorandum of Agreement and closing documents were finalized, yet Dillon and his lawyer delayed the closing, without explanation, until the end of December. Although Dillon had the right under the Memorandum of Agreement to choose a date as late as the end of December, his prior eagerness to close, along with the fact that the closing documents had been finalized in the summer, suggest that the delay may have had something to do with financial distress and a plan to misrepresent Dillon's distressed financial status.

One of the documents on the privilege logs concerns the "Dillon mortgage" and an "update re: Dynamo financing and selection of closing date." Dillon and Hanson communicated about a mortgage obtained by Dillon before or during July YR-3. Yet neither of Dillon's personal financial statements reflect any mortgage on Dillon's primary and secondary residences. If Dillon mortgaged his property in consultation with his lawyer, there is a reasonable basis to believe Dillon's communications with his lawyer on these subjects may show he was planning fraud when the documents were created.

Moreover, two documents referenced on the privilege log are for payment of past legal services indicating late payment of Hanson's fees. These letters are further described in the privilege log as concerning "Dynamo payment due at closing" and "capital sources," suggesting that, in conjunction with late payments, Dillon was possibly in financial distress; these communications with his attorney may show he was planning fraud at this time.

Finally, immediately before the closing, Hanson and Dillon communicated by email and letter three times about the personal financial statement. Importantly, the log indicates an "approval of personal financial statement." Given the proximity of these documents to the actual closing, there is a reasonable basis to believe that Dillon communicated with Hanson for the purpose of perpetrating a fraud by providing a false financial statement at closing. The nonprivileged evidence supports this argument. On the day before closing, after the email communications between Dillon and Hanson, Hanson represented to Paul's attorney, Jamie Norris, that he personally reviewed the closing documents, including the financial statement, and represented that they were "fine" and had them delivered to Norris. As Paul states in her declaration in support of this motion, Dillon described Hanson as knowledgeable of his business and finances. It was Hanson who drafted the asset purchase agreement and knew Dillon's obligations at closing. It was Hanson who personally prepared, reviewed, and delivered the financial statement and closing documents and assured that they were fine. For purposes of the attorney-client communications, it is Dillon's intent that is at issue. The letter and emails communications in the days immediately preceding the closing may show that Dillon was using Hanson's services as his attorney to facilitate the fraud.

U.S. v. Boender also supports in camera review of the emails and letters exchanged between Dillon and Hanson relating to Dillon's financial condition and the financial statements that Hanson gave to Paul. *U.S. v. Boender*, 639 F.3d 650 (7th Cir. 2011). Arguably, *Boender* also supports an in camera hearing in order for the court to question Hanson. *Boender* involved a grand-jury inquiry in a public corruption case. Boender gave his defense attorney a false invoice that helped his case. The attorney questioned whether the invoice was genuine, and Boender assured him that it was. The defense attorney then provided the false invoice to the prosecution. Boender was charged with obstruction of justice based upon the production of the invoice. At trial, the prosecution sought to introduce testimony about the false invoice. It argued that any communication between Boender and his attorney regarding the production of the false invoice was not privileged because those conversations fell within the crime-fraud exception. The trial court correctly conducted an in camera hearing of Boender's defense attorney. The court had ample evidence to conclude the invoice was false and the only way for the court to determine how the invoice got into the defense counsel's hand and whether Boender intended the false invoice to be given to the government was through the testimony of his counsel. Here, Hanson delivered a false financial statement to Paul's attorney, representing that it was fine. As in *Boender*, the only way to determine how Hanson received the financial statements and whether Dillon intended them to be conveyed to Paul is through the court examining the correspondence and possibly interviewing Hanson.

Given that Paul can make the required showing, the court should exercise its discretion to conduct an in camera review of the documents. First, there are eight documents at issue—a small number that would not be burdensome for the court to review. Second, the documents are important to the case because the fraudulent inducement claims require proof of intent to defraud. While the financial statements and Hanson's email standing alone may provide circumstantial evidence of intent to defraud, the emails containing the communications with Dillon and a possible interview with Hanson are a far stronger source on this issue. Third, there is a strong likelihood that Paul's nonprivileged evidence, along with the evidence produced through the in camera review, will establish that the crime-fraud exception does apply.

A's should anticipate concerns by the trial court regarding the timing of the motion. The motion is being brought when only minimal discovery has occurred. As discussed above, while other discovery may provide circumstantial evidence of Dillon's intent to commit fraud and his use of Hanson's advice to do so, the letters and emails in the privilege log will likely reveal that intent more directly. Additionally, whether Paul has met her burden at the in camera hearing may inform Paul and Dillon's further decisions on the merits of Paul's fraud claim, perhaps expediting resolution by the parties on this claim.

B. The Prima Facie Showing

The evidence produced through the in camera review, together with the non-privileged information contained in the Paul's exhibits accompanying her motion, will likewise establish a prima facie showing that the crime-fraud exception applies. Paul need only show a reasonable basis to suspect that 1) Dillon was committing or intending to commit a fraud, and 2) that his communications with Hanson were used in furtherance of that fraud. *In re Grand Jury*, 705 F.3d 133 (3d Cir. 2012). The documents in the period following the signing of the asset purchase agreement and up to the closing reveal Dillon to be a man in financial distress and consulting with his attorney about the upcoming closing. His attorney Hanson was fully knowledgeable about Dillon's business and finances. After communicating with Dillon, Hanson took responsibility for the personal review of the financial statement and delivered the financial statement to Paul's attorney, representing that it was "fine," yet the financial statement was identical to the March financial statement. The requirements of NITA for a prima facie case have been met.

V. POSSIBLE ARGUMENTS FOR DILLON AND DYNAMO

A. Threshold Showing

Plaintiff Michelle Paul fails to meet the *Zolin* standard. She does not show "a factual basis adequate to support a good faith belief by a reasonable person" that in camera review may reveal evidence to establish application of the crime fraud exception. Paul argues that certain entries on the privilege log suggest financial difficulties by Dillon. Discovery has only just commenced as to Dillon's finances. Nevertheless, Paul surmises, based on these entries, that Dillon may have asked his attorney, Hanson, for advice on planning to create a false financial statement for purposes of closing and that Hanson may have given such advice. Some speculation can occur at the threshold stage. Nothing in the privilege log, however, suggests that such requests for legal advice in furtherance of fraudulent activity were made or that such advice was given. At this point, Paul raises only a "sneaking suspicion." For advice to be used "in furtherance" of the fraud, the client must intend that the advice advance the fraudulent purpose. The advice cannot merely "relate" to the fraud. At best, Paul can only show that these documents may be relevant to her fraudulent inducement claim, but relevance is inadequate to establish the crime-fraud exception.

As to the later entries on the privilege log, Paul emphasizes, that Hanson stated he reviewed the closing documents, delivered them to her attorney, and represented that they were fine. But because only very limited discovery has occurred, Paul has not even established the premise for her "sneaking suspicion" that the December 29, YR-3, financial statement was substantively false as to Dillon's net worth. Because the privilege belongs to the client, it is Dillon's intent, not Hanson's, that is at issue. Even assuming for discussion that there were errors in the details of the financial statement, there is no basis to believe that Hanson's legal advice had anything to do with them. At this point, so early in discovery, it is only speculation that Dillon used Hanson to facilitate a fraud, and indeed, whether a fraud even occurred.

Moreover, this motion is premature. In describing the court's exercise of discretion to conduct an in camera review, *U.S. v. Zolin* stated that the court could consider "the likelihood that the evidence produced through in camera review, *together with other available evidence then before the court*, will establish that the crime-fraud exception does apply." *Zolin*, at 572 (emphasis added). It is premature to consider a request for in camera review of privileged documents when only minimal discovery has taken place. Paul suspects that otherwise protected communications with counsel were intended to facilitate a fraud, without yet having gathered the nonprivileged evidence on the issue. Witness depositions have not yet taken place. The request for financial records and other documents has only just begun. On the current record, there are insufficient facts demonstrating the applicability of the crime fraud exception to warrant in camera review. As a result, there is an insufficient factual basis, as required by *Zolin* at the threshold stage, to conclude that review of the emails sought by Paul may reveal evidence to establish that the crime fraud exception applies.

For this reason, *United States v. Boender* has no applicability here because we are in the infancy of discovery. In *Boender*, at the time of the in camera review, the government had already indicted Boender and had ample evidence that he falsified the invoice. The only question was how the prosecutor could present this evidence at trial; the government needed the attorney to relate conversations with Boender, which could not occur if the court determined that the attorney-client privilege applied. The *Boender* case distinguishes between situations in which a case is still being investigated, as in *Zolin*, and a case in which there is already sufficient evidence to indict the defendant. The circumstances here are more like *Zolin*. Also, even if the court were to entertain the applicability of *Boender*, the opinion states that "where the disputed communications are contained in documents, the best course may often be review by the judge alone in camera." In *Boender*, there was no document.

As to the issue of prematurity of the in camera review, Paul may argue that an early in camera review is the most expedient and efficient way to determine Dillon's intent. But an in camera review is still an intrusion on the attorney-client privilege. The privilege is enforced to encourage full and frank communication between attorneys and their clients. Court findings that could potentially deprive the client of that significant protection should be based on an adequate record and not short-circuited for efficiency. Paul brings her motion, with the ultimate goal to pierce the veil of attorney-client communications, at a very early phase of the pretrial proceedings, when almost no discovery has even taken place. Paul seeks access to privileged documents without first exploring whether she can discover this same information through nonprivileged sources.

Zolin states that the court may "defer its in camera review if it concludes that additional evidence in support of the crime-fraud exception may be available that is not allegedly privileged, and that production of the additional evidence will not unduly disrupt or delay the proceedings." *Id.* at 572. Such a course of action is proper here.

B. Prima Facie Showing

Because Paul cannot make the threshold showing, she cannot make the higher prima facie showing. At this point, so early in the discovery process, the in camera review would occur on the basis of the following documents: eight emails and letters for which the claim of privilege is asserted, Paul's memo, two financial statements, and an email from Hanson to Norris. These materials are not adequate to supply the court with a reasonable basis to suspect 1) that Dillon was committing or intending to commit a fraud, and 2) that the attorney-client communication was used in furtherance of that alleged fraud, so as to break the seal of secrecy. Paul has not met the reasonable basis standard. That standard is "reasonably demanding" and "neither speculation nor evidence that shows only a distant likelihood of corruption is enough." *In re Grand Jury*, 705 F.3d 133 (3d Cir. 2012).

VI. CASE LAW (REDACTED VERSIONS)

A. *United States v. Zolin*, 491 U.S. 554 (1989)

This case arises out of the efforts of the Criminal Investigation Division of the Internal Revenue Service (IRS) to investigate the tax returns of L. Ron Hubbard, founder of the Church of Scientology (the Church), for the calendar years 1979 through 1983. We granted certiorari . . . to consider two issues that have divided the Courts of Appeals.

* * *

[Discussion of first issue omitted.] The second issue concerns the testimonial privilege for attorney-client communications and, more particularly, the generally recognized exception to that privilege for communications in furtherance of future illegal conduct—the so-called "crime-fraud" exception. The specific question presented is whether the applicability of the crime-fraud exception must be established by "independent evidence" (i.e., without reference to the content of the contested communications themselves), or, alternatively, whether the applicability of that exception can be resolved by an in camera inspection of the allegedly privileged material. We reject the "independent evidence" approach and hold that the district court, under circumstances we explore below, and at the behest of the party opposing the claim of privilege, may conduct an in camera review of the materials in question.

* * *

Questions of privilege that arise in the course of the adjudication of federal rights are "governed by the principles of the common law as they may be interpreted by the courts of the United States in the light of reason and experience." Fed.Rule Evid. 501. We have recognized the attorney-client privilege under federal law, as "the oldest of the privileges for confidential communications known to the common law." *Upjohn Co. v. United States*, 449 U.S. 383, 389, (1981). Although the underlying rationale for the privilege has changed over time, courts long have viewed its central concern as one "to encourage full and frank communication between attorneys and their clients and thereby promote broader public interests in the observance of law and administration of justice." *Upjohn*, 449 U.S., at 389, 101 S.Ct., at 682. That purpose, of course, requires that clients be free to "make full disclosure to their attorneys" of past wrongdoings, *Fisher v. United States*, 425 U.S. 391, 403, (1976), in order that the client may obtain "the aid of persons having knowledge of the law and skilled in its practice," *Hunt v. Blackburn*, 128 U.S. 464, 470 (1888).

The attorney-client privilege is not without its costs. Cf. *Trammel v. United States*, 445 U.S. 40, 50 (1980). "[S]ince the privilege has the effect of withholding relevant information from the factfinder, it applies only where necessary to achieve its purpose." *Fisher*, 425 U.S., at 403. The attorney-client privilege must necessarily protect the confidences of wrongdoers, but the reason for that protection—the centrality of open client and attorney communication to the proper functioning of our adversary system of justice—"ceas[es] to operate at a certain point, namely, where the desired advice refers not to prior wrongdoing, but to future wrongdoing." 8 Wigmore, § 2298, p. 573 (emphasis in original); see also *Clark v. United States*, 289 U.S. 1 (1933). It is the purpose of the crime-fraud exception to the attorney-client privilege to assure that the "seal of secrecy," *ibid.*, between lawyer and client does not extend to communications "made for the purpose of getting advice for the commission of a fraud" or crime. *O'Rourke v. Darbishire*, [1920] A.C. 581, 604 (P.C.).

* * *

A variety of questions may arise when a party raises the crime-fraud exception. The parties to this case have not been in complete agreement as to which of these questions are presented here. In an effort to clarify the matter, we observe, first, that we need not decide the quantum of proof necessary ultimately to establish the applicability of the crime-fraud exception. Rather, we are concerned here with the type of evidence that may be used to make that ultimate showing. . . . [T]he initial question in this case is whether a district court, at the request of the party opposing the privilege, may review the allegedly privileged communications in camera to determine whether the crime-fraud exception applies. If such in camera review is permitted, the second question we must consider is whether some threshold evidentiary showing is needed before the district court may undertake the requested review. Finally, if a threshold showing is required, we must consider the type of evidence the opposing party may use to meet it:

* * *

We consider first the question whether a district court may ever honor the request of the party opposing the privilege to conduct an in camera review of allegedly privileged communications to determine whether those communications fall within the crime-fraud exception. We conclude that no express provision of the Federal Rules of Evidence bars such use of in camera review and that it would be unwise to prohibit it in all instances as a matter of federal common law.

* * *

We turn to the question whether in camera review at the behest of the party asserting the crime-fraud exception is always permissible, or, in contrast, whether the party seeking in camera review must make some threshold showing that such review is appropriate. In addressing this question, we attend to the detrimental effect, if any, of in camera review on the policies underlying the privilege and on the orderly administration of justice in our courts. We conclude that some such showing must be made.

* * *

A blanket rule allowing in camera review as a tool for determining the applicability of the crime-fraud exception . . . would place the policy of protecting open and legitimate disclosure between attorneys and clients at undue risk. There is also reason to be concerned about the possible due process implications of routine use of in camera proceedings. See, e.g., *In re John Doe Corp.*, 675 F.2d 482, 489–490 (CA2 1982); *In re Special September 1978 Grand Jury*, 640 F.2d 49, 56–58 (CA7 1980). Finally, we cannot ignore the burdens in camera review places upon the district courts, which may well be required to evaluate large evidentiary records without open adversarial guidance by the parties.

There is no reason to permit opponents of the privilege to engage in groundless fishing expeditions, with the district courts as their unwitting (and perhaps unwilling) agents. Courts of Appeals have suggested that in camera review is available to evaluate claims of crime or fraud only "when justified," *In re John Doe Corp.*, 675 F.2d, at 490, or "[i]n appropriate cases," *In re Sealed Case*, 676 F.2d 793, 815 (1982) (opinion of Wright, J.). Indeed, the Government conceded at oral argument (albeit reluctantly) that a district court would be mistaken if it reviewed documents in camera solely because "the government beg[ged it]" to do so, "with no reason to suspect crime or fraud." Tr. of Oral Arg. 26; see also id., at 60. We agree.

In fashioning a standard for determining when in camera review is appropriate, we begin with the observation that "in camera inspection . . . is a smaller intrusion upon the confidentiality of the attorney-client relationship than is public disclosure." Fried, Too High a Price for Truth: The Exception to the Attorney–Client Privilege for Contemplated Crimes and Frauds, 64 N.C.L.Rev. 443, 467 (1986). We therefore conclude that a lesser evidentiary showing is needed to trigger in camera review than is required ultimately to overcome the privilege. *Ibid.* The threshold we set, in other words, need not be a stringent one.

We think that the following standard strikes the correct balance. Before engaging in in camera review to determine the applicability of the crime-fraud exception, "the judge should require a showing of a factual basis adequate to support a good faith belief by a reasonable person," *Caldwell v. District Court*, 644 P.2d 26, 33 (Colo. 1982), that in camera review of the materials may reveal evidence to establish the claim that the crime-fraud exception applies.

Once that showing is made, the decision whether to engage in *in camera* review rests in the sound discretion of the district court. The court should make that decision in light of the facts and circumstances of the particular case, including, among other things, the volume of materials the district court has been asked to review, the relative importance to the case of the alleged privileged information, and the likelihood that the evidence produced through in camera review, together with other available evidence then before the court, will establish that the crime-fraud exception does apply. The district court is also free to defer its in camera review if it concludes that additional evidence in support of the crime-fraud exception may be available that is not allegedly privileged, and that production of the additional evidence will not unduly disrupt or delay the proceedings.

* * *

The question remains as to what kind of evidence a district court may consider in determining whether it has the discretion to undertake an in camera review of an allegedly privileged communication at the behest of the party opposing the privilege. . . . We conclude that the party opposing the privilege may use any nonprivileged evidence in support of its request for in camera review. . . .

We hold that in camera review may be used to determine whether allegedly privileged attorney-client communications fall within the crime-fraud exception. We further hold, however, that before a district court may engage in in camera review at the request of the party opposing the privilege, that party must present evidence sufficient to support a reasonable belief that in camera review may yield evidence that establishes the exception's applicability. Finally, we hold that the threshold showing to obtain in camera review may be met by using any relevant evidence, lawfully obtained, that has not been adjudicated to be privileged.

B. *In re Grand Jury Investigation,* 974 F.2d 1068 (9th Cir. 1992)

Excerpt

It is well settled that the attorney-client privilege does not extend to attorney-client communications which solicit or offer advice for the commission of a crime or fraud. In *United States v. Zolin,* 491 U.S. 554, 565, the Supreme Court held that *in camera* review of privileged information may be used to establish whether the crime-fraud exception applies. The Court set forth a two-step analysis for determining whether *in camera* review is appropriate in a given case. First, there must be a minimal showing that the crime-fraud exception could apply. *Id.* at 572. If this initial hurdle is overcome, then the district court has the discretion to conduct an *in camera* review. *Id.*

The first step in the *Zolin* analysis sets the threshold for the evidentiary showing necessary before a court can conduct *in camera* review. In establishing the standard, the Court recognized that *in camera* review of documents is a much smaller intrusion on the attorney-client privilege than full disclosure: "The threshold we set, in other words, need not be a stringent one. We think that the following standard strikes the correct balance. Before engaging in *in camera* review to determine the applicability of the crime-fraud exception, 'the judge should require a showing of a factual basis adequate to support a good faith belief by a reasonable person,'" that *in camera* review of the materials may reveal evidence to establish the claim that the crime-fraud exception applies. 491 U.S. at 572.

The Court in *Zolin* also set forth several factors to guide district courts in exercising their discretion in conducting *in camera* review. Once the threshold showing is made to allow *in camera* review, courts should make the decision to review in light of the amount of material they have been asked to review, the relevance of the alleged privilege material to the case, and the likelihood that *in camera* review will reveal evidence to establish the applicability of the crime-fraud exception. 491 U.S. at 572.

To the extent that the district court held that the government's showing did not meet the *Zolin* threshold because it required the court to engage in "speculation," the court misapplied *Zolin*. Some speculation is required under the *Zolin* threshold. *In camera* review is appropriate as long as the showing supports a reasonable belief "that in camera review of the materials *may* reveal *evidence* to establish the claim that the crime-fraud exception applies." 491 U.S. [554], 572, (emphasis added). A *prima facie* showing of crime-fraud is not required before an in camera inspection is appropriate. 491 U.S. at 563 n. 7. A showing sufficient to establish a reasonable belief that in camera review may lead to evidence that the exception applies is enough to allow in camera review. The *Zolin* threshold is designed to prevent "groundless fishing expeditions," not to prevent all speculation by the district court. 491 U.S. at 571.

Moreover, *Zolin* requires only a factual showing sufficient to support a reasonable, good-faith belief that review of the privileged documents *"may reveal* evidence to establish the claim that the crime-fraud exception applies." 491 U.S. at 572. (emphasis added). The district court, however, apparently required a factual showing that supports a good-faith belief that the crime-fraud exception applies. Such a standard is set too high. There is an important difference between showing how documents may supply evidence that the crime-fraud exception applies and showing directly that the exception applies. This difference results in a considerably lower threshold for conducting in camera review than for fully disclosing documents.

C. *In re Grand Jury*, 705 F.3d 133 (3d Cir. 2012)

Excerpt

[U]nder the crime-fraud exception, the party seeking to overcome the privilege . . . "must make a prima facie showing that (1) the client was committing or intending to commit a fraud or crime, and (2) the attorney-client communications were in furtherance of that alleged crime or fraud." *In re Grand Jury*

Subpoena, 223 F.3d at 217 (citations omitted). The "prima facie" standard is drawn from the Supreme Court's decision in *Clark v. United States*, 289 U.S. 1, which stated in part," To drive the privilege away, there must be something to give colour to the charge; there must be prima facie evidence that it has some foundation in fact." *Id.* at 15. While there is general agreement on these precepts, courts of appeals are divided as to the appropriate quantum of proof necessary to make a prima facie showing.

* * *

Today, we clarify that our precedent is properly captured by the reasonable basis standard.

* * *

Where there is a reasonable basis to suspect that the privilege holder was committing or intending to commit a crime or fraud and that the attorney-client communications or attorney work product were used in furtherance of the alleged crime or fraud, this is enough to break the privilege. The reasonable basis standard "is intended to be reasonably demanding; neither speculation nor evidence that shows only a distant likelihood of corruption is enough." *In re Grand Jury Proceedings*, 417 F.3d 18, 23 (1st Cir. 2005). At the same time, the party opposing the privilege is not required to introduce evidence sufficient to support a verdict of crime or fraud or even to show that it is more likely than not that the crime or fraud occurred. See *id.* at 22; *In re Grand Jury Investigation*, 445 F.3d 266, 274–75 (3d. Cir. 2006.)

* * *

D.   *United States v. Boender*, 639 F.3d 650 (7th Cir. 2011)

Footnotes omitted

Over the course of 2004, Calvin Boender spent approximately $38,000 on home repairs for Isaac Carothers, a Chicago Alderman and crucial player in Boender's attempt to have certain industrial property rezoned for commercial and residential development. Boender also convinced a couple of business associates to donate, at his expense, to Carothers's aunt's congressional campaign. And when the government investigated the earlier events, Boender fabricated an invoice for the home repairs, purportedly sent from his general contractor to Carothers. As a result, Boender was indicted, tried, and convicted of bribing a local official, exceeding federal campaign contribution limits through straw-man donations, and endeavoring to obstruct justice. He appeals aspects of all his convictions. We affirm.

I.   Background

A. The Galewood Yards Rezoning

In 2000, Boender purchased a 50-acre parcel in northwest Chicago's Armitage Industrial Corridor. The property, known as Galewood Yards, was zoned for manufacturing use and largely undeveloped. For four years, Union Pacific Railroad leased all, and then part, of the property. Things changed in early 2004 when Union Pacific left. Boender began searching for other uses for the land, and eventually decided to build a full-service retail and residential community. But the City of Chicago's Department of Planning and Development had other plans for the property and, at about the same time, was attempting to designate the entire industrial corridor a Planned Manufacturing District (PMD). This "zoning overlay" would lock in the manufacturing designation for the property, making it very difficult to change the zoning once the PMD was in place.

Local politics being what they are, neither change was likely to succeed without the support of the local alderman. Mindful of this reality, Boender attempted throughout 2004 to cultivate the support of Carothers, the alderman whose ward covered the largest part of Galewood Yards. . . . In June, Boender hired Stanley Walczak, a general contractor with whom he had previously worked, to paint various parts of Alderman Carothers's house. Boender arranged to pay for the work. When Boender learned of the Department's plan to establish a PMD that included Galewood Yards, he was "irate" and told a Department representative that he did not need to deal with her because "he had made a deal with the alderman." And when the same representative spoke to Carothers about the plan, [Carothers] responded that "he was going to do what he wanted to do with the land in his ward and [she] was not to discuss it with anybody." Nevertheless, the mayor approved the Department's plan. Early in July, Boender and Carothers met with the Department to discuss the future of Galewood Yards and advocate rezoning the property for residential and retail use, but the Department remained opposed.

While painting Carothers's house in July, Walczak's crew discovered that the windows were rotting. Carothers selected expensive windows, and Boender authorized Walczak to install 31 windows, telling him that Carothers had "helped him a great deal with changing the zoning of Galewood Yards." Boender paid for the windows with a check for $11,252 written from one of his companies. In August, Boender also received an offer from Kerasotes Theatres to purchase 10 acres of Galewood Yards for approximately $4.8 million, contingent on a zoning change to allow for commercial use. That same month, Alderman Carothers gave an interview to the Chicago Sun–Times, at Boender's request, speaking in favor of rezoning Galewood Yards. At about the same time, Carothers asked Walczak to replace several doors and perform some other interior repair work in his house. Boender told Walczak to "Go ahead and do it. The guy is worth it."

In September, Boender filed an application for a zoning change with the City Council. Two weeks later, he paid $12,800 for two air conditioning units for Carothers's home. Shortly after that, Boender authorized Walczak to do additional work necessary to install the units, explaining that the alderman "had helped him a lot with the change of zoning" and "went so far as to stand up to Mayor Daley." In October, Boender paid $13,350 for this work. All told, Boender paid approximately $38,000 for repairs and improvements to Carothers's home.

Although the home repairs were complete in October, the matter of the Galewood Yards zoning was still open. Unable to proceed with the PMD designation of Galewood Yards without the support of Carothers, the City agreed to a compromise. In 2005, it helped secure an industrial use for half of the property and in exchange agreed to support the rezoning of the other half of the property for commercial and residential use. Carothers sent the Department an official letter of support for the compromise in February 2006. . . . In accordance with the compromise, Carothers supported the ordinance rezoning Galewood Yards, and it passed the City Council on March 29.

B. The Fabricated Invoice

A year later, in August 2007, Boender and Walczak received grand jury subpoenas. They met several times to get their stories straight. After discussing different options, they settled on a story that Walczak had initially billed Carothers but when Carothers failed to pay, Boender felt obliged to pay the bill because he had given Walczak the job. In January 2008, the government issued more grand jury subpoenas to Boender's companies, including those from which the checks for Carothers's home repairs were written. Boender then asked a business partner how much had been spent on the home repairs; when he learned the total amount, Boender stated that he "wish[ed] we had sent an invoice out to the alderman for the work." He then fabricated an invoice for $38,000, dated September 8, 2004, and supposedly from Historic Homes, Ltd., a defunct company he had previously owned.

In late February, Boender gave the fake invoice to his real estate attorney, Michael O'Connor, informing him that the invoice was covered by the subpoena and that he wanted to produce it to the government. O'Connor's only role was to forward Boender's documents to criminal defense attorney Dan Reidy, with whom Boender and O'Connor initially met on February 25. After the initial conversation, Reidy scheduled a meeting with the government to discuss the case and put Boender's best argument forward.

During their initial conversation, Boender had told Reidy that he had sent an invoice to Carothers for work done in 2004. But when Reidy reviewed the invoice in preparation for his meeting with the government, he called Boender and expressed concern that "perhaps the invoice hadn't actually been sent to Mr. Carothers because [he] noticed it was typed and that it was an original." He also told Boender that because Historic Homes was not subject to a subpoena, they did not yet have to produce it. Boender asked whether the document would help him; when Reidy responded that "if it was real, it helped him," Boender assured him that it was in fact real.

At the February 27 meeting, prosecutors told Reidy that the invoice might not be genuine. On February 29, however, the invoice was Bates-stamped and produced with other responsive material. Later that day, Reidy sent an e-mail with Boender's authorization informing the government that the invoice "was not prepared on or about the September 8, 2004 date it bears and was not sent to the named addressee."

C. Criminal Proceedings

In 2009, the grand jury indicted Boender on various charges, including . . . corruptly giving things of value to a local official in violation of 18 U.S.C. § 666(a)(2) by paying for Carothers's home repairs; and endeavoring to obstruct justice in violation of 18 U.S.C. § 1503(a) by asking Walczak to give a false story to the government and fabricating and intending to produce a false invoice in support of that story.

In February 2010, the government moved in limine to admit [at trial] testimony and evidence concerning the production of the fabricated invoice, contending that communications about document production are not privileged. It also argued that any privilege that did exist was forfeited under the crime-fraud exception, and asked the district court to conduct, if necessary, an in camera hearing to determine whether the exception applied. Boender simultaneously moved to exclude any testimony or evidence related to Reidy because it was protected by the attorney-client privilege. In response, the district court held an in camera hearing to resolve the issue. It directed Reidy to appear and ruled that both Boender and the government could attend the hearing. The court heard testimony from Reidy, Reidy's staff, and O'Connor. Finding sufficient evidence that the conversations at issue were "not for the purpose of obtaining legal advice but for the purpose of perpetrating a crime in connection with the grand jury investigation," and that Boender used his attorneys "as 'front men' in a scheme to subvert the judicial process," the court granted the government's motion to admit the evidence.

Over the course of a six-day trial, the jury heard testimony from numerous witnesses, including Boender's partner and his bookkeeper, from Walczak, . . . and from attorneys O'Connor and Reidy. The jury convicted Boender on all counts. . . .

II. Law & Analysis

On appeal, Boender challenges . . . his conviction under 18 U.S.C. § 1503 on the grounds that the district court erred in admitting attorney-client privileged communications under the crime-fraud exception. . . .

* * *

B. Obstruction of Justice

Boender . . . challenges his conviction for obstruction of justice under 18 U.S.C. § 1503, claiming that it was based on inadmissible attorney-client privileged communications. Here, he argues that the district court erred in admitting testimony from his former defense attorney based on the crime-fraud exception to the attorney-client privilege. We review a district court's application of the crime-fraud exception for an abuse of discretion. *United States v. BDO Seidman, LLP*, 492 F.3d 806, 818 (7th Cir. 2007).

The crime-fraud exception helps to ensure that the attorney-client privilege does not protect communications made "in furtherance of a crime or fraud." *United States v. Zolin*, 491 U.S. 554, 563 (1989); *BDO Seidman*, 492 F.3d at 818. To establish the crime-fraud exception, and thus defeat the privilege, the government must "present prima facie evidence that gives color to the charge by showing some foundation in fact." *BDO Seidman*, 492 F.3d at 818. . . . The court may, if necessary, examine the privileged communications themselves to determine whether they further a crime or fraud, so long as there is a "showing of a factual basis adequate to support a good faith belief by a reasonable person that in camera review of the materials may reveal evidence to establish the claim that the crime-fraud exception applies." *Zolin*, 491 U.S. at 572.

Boender challenges the procedures the district court followed in deciding that the crime-fraud exception applies. He argues that there was not enough evidence to justify the district court's decision to hold an in camera hearing in the first place. . . .

We begin with the district court's decision to hold an in camera hearing to receive testimony related to the crime-fraud exception. Boender's argument on this first point is difficult to follow—he appears to conflate the evidence required to establish a prima facie case supporting the crime-fraud exception with the evidence required to justify in camera review. The rule allowing for in camera review does not presuppose any particular quantum of evidence establishing the appropriateness of the exception itself, merely enough evidence to support a "good faith belief by a reasonable person" that such review may reveal evidence establishing the exception. *Id.* In other words, would in camera examination of Boender's defense attorney answer open questions regarding whether the attorney-client communications were made in furtherance of an endeavor to obstruct justice?

The answer to that question is clearly yes. Boender's argument to the contrary ignores a substantial amount of evidence. Specifically, before the hearing the government had evidence that Boender expressed a wish that he had invoiced Carothers back in 2004; that his bookkeeper had not prepared such an invoice; that he had discussed the existence of such an invoice with his defense attorney just before his attorney met with the prosecutor; and that his defense attorney had produced an apparently fake invoice, backdated to September 8, 2004, and sent by a defunct company. The district court had ample reason to believe that the missing pieces to the puzzle—how the document got into the defense attorney's hands in the first place and whether Boender intended the document to be discussed with and produced to the government—could only be found in the testimony of Boender's attorneys. The district court was justified in holding an in camera hearing.

* * *

As we noted above, there was ample evidence to suggest that an in camera hearing would help clarify whether the crime-fraud exception would apply. The district court noted the strength of the evidence the government presented in its detailed proffer, but rather than decide whether the crime-fraud exception applied on the basis of that evidence alone, it ordered an in camera hearing. This is not a case of the government fishing for clues amid otherwise privileged information; rather, the purpose was to confirm what was strongly suggested by the evidence, that the crime-fraud exception would apply.

* * *

[In addressing who may be present during the in camera hearing "when the source of the evidence is live testimony," the court in *Boender* observed: "Where the disputed communications are contained in documents . . . the best course may often be review by the judge alone in camera."]

* * *

Finally, for completeness, we note that Boender at times appears to advance [another] argument: even after the district court heard Reidy's testimony at the in camera hearing, there was insufficient evidence to establish a prima facie case that the initial conversation was in furtherance of a crime. He argues that what occurred at that meeting was at most "anticipatory" obstruction of justice: no decisions were made at that point on whether to turn over the fake invoice, and the discussions of the invoice were purely "hypothetical." Not only is this argument virtually undeveloped, it is a nonstarter. According to Reidy, he and Boender discussed Reidy meeting with the government to present Boender in the most favorable light, as an extortion victim rather than a criminal, and thus improve Boender's situation with the government. They spent considerable time going over the facts of the case, so that Reidy could put forward the best argument for this position. In this context, Boender told Reidy that Carothers had been sent an invoice for the home repairs. On the morning of the meeting with the government, and after he had reviewed the original invoice, Reidy spoke with Boender and expressed concern over whether the invoice had actually been sent to Carothers. Boender assured Reidy that it had been sent. Boender meant for Reidy to communicate his false story, including the existence of the invoice, to the government. Whether or not Boender actually intended, or agreed, that Reidy produce the invoice itself is irrelevant. The government's proffer gave more than enough "color to the charge" that Boender's communications with Reidy regarding the existence and authenticity of the invoice were in furtherance of his endeavor to obstruct justice by conveying false information to the government and influencing the ongoing grand-jury investigation.

III. Conclusion

None of Boender's challenges to his convictions succeeds. . . . The district court did not abuse its discretion in holding an *in camera* hearing on the crime-fraud exception. . . . Therefore, the district court's judgment is Affirmed.

Three: Preliminary Injunctions— Trade Secrets

I. Exercises

A. Motion for Preliminary Injunction without Live Testimony

B's for the Defendants, Dynamo Sporting Goods and Arthur Dillon

Argue for Dynamo and Dillon in support of their motion for preliminary injunction which sought the following:

1) An immediate return of the customer list alleged to constitute trade secrets;

2) An order enjoining Paul, her company, employees, and agents from using these trade secrets;

3) An order enjoining Paul, her company, employees, and agents from soliciting Sportslifeware's customers;

4) An order enjoining Paul from recruiting and hiring Sportslifeware's employees.

The motion for preliminary injunction requests all of the above relief. In your argument, you are free to focus on one or more of the arguments.

A's for the Plaintiff, Paul

Argue in opposition to the above motion for a preliminary injunction.

Supporting Materials

In preparing their arguments, both sides may rely on i) documents and correspondence contained in the case file; ii) the key cases, Memorandum of Law, and materials contained in the attached library; iii) the statements distributed during the program, which shall be considered depositions. For the purposes of this exercise, assume that all of the pleadings contained in the case file have been filed and served. Possible arguments for each side are contained in the memorandum. You are not required to use these arguments nor are you limited to these arguments.

Please do not conduct additional legal research. You should read the attached "key cases" and may rely on the cases cited in the memorandum of law. However, do not read any of the cases cited in those materials. Also, during argument, you may not argue other cases that you may know about. In other words, your universe of law is contained in the materials that follow.

B. Motion for Preliminary Injunction with Live Testimony

B's for the Defendants, Dynamo Sporting Goods and Arthur Dillon

In this exercise, conduct a direct examination of Arthur Dillon and Pat Hingle in support of your motion. Other members of the B group will play Arthur Dillon and Pat Hingle for you. You will have the opportunity to cross-examine Michelle Paul when the A's call her.

Argue for Dynamo and Dillon in support of a motion which seeks the following relief:

> 1) An immediate return of the customer lists alleged to constitute trade secrets;
>
> 2) An order enjoining Paul, her company, employees, and agents from using these trade secrets;
>
> 3) An order enjoining Paul, her company, employees, and agents from soliciting Sportslifeware's customers;
>
> 4) An order enjoining Paul from recruiting and hiring Sportslifeware's employees.

In your argument, you are free to focus on one or more of the above arguments.

A's for the Plaintiff, Paul

Conduct a direct examination of Michelle Paul and J.J. Lyons. Other members of the A group will play Michelle Paul and J.J. Lyons for you. You will also have the opportunity to cross-examine Dillon and Hingle when the B's call them. Argue in opposition to the above motion for a preliminary injunction.

Supporting Materials

In preparing their arguments, both sides may rely on i) documents and correspondence contained in the case file; ii) the key cases, Memorandum of Law, and materials contained in the attached library; iii) the statements distributed during the program, which shall be considered depositions. For the purposes of this exercise, assume that all of the pleadings contained in the case file have been filed and served. Possible arguments for each side are contained in the memorandum. You are not required to use these arguments nor are you limited to these arguments.

> **Please do not conduct additional legal research. You should read the attached "key cases" and may rely on the cases cited in the memorandum of law. However, do not read any of the cases cited in those materials. Also, during argument, you may not argue other cases that you may know about. In other words, your universe of law is contained in the materials that follow.**

II. Memorandum of Law

TO: PAUL V. DYNAMO FILE
FROM: ASSOCIATE
RE: MOTION FOR PRELIMINARY INJUNCTION

A. Factual Background

Dillon and Dynamo seek a preliminary injunction ordering the immediate return of the customer lists alleged to constitute trade secrets; enjoining Paul, her company, employees, and agents from using these trade secrets; and enjoining Paul, her company, employees, and agents from soliciting Sportslifeware's customers and recruiting and hiring Sportslifeware's employees. Immediately after Paul filed her complaint, Dynamo and Dillon asked for temporary and permanent injunctive relief. A hearing on the temporary restraining order request was held, and the request was denied. Expedited discovery was ordered, and the preliminary injunction request was set. Depositions of Michelle Paul, J.J. Lyons, Arthur Dillon, and Pat Hingle have been held, and some document discovery has been completed.

Dillon and Dynamo's Counterclaim to Paul's original complaint alleges breach of contract, fraud in the inducement and unfair competition. These claims center upon Section 5 of the Asset Purchase Agreement, which provides covenants of confidentiality and trade secret protection running from Paul as the seller to Dillon and Dynamo as the buyer. Specifically, the Agreement requires Paul to refrain from disclosing confidential information and trade secrets or obtaining or using confidential information and trade secrets of the business in any other business, operations, or activities. Trade secrets are broadly defined as any compilation that provides a competitive advantage to the business and the Asset Purchase Agreement specifically includes a "specialized customer list" within its definition of trade secrets. Under the agreement, trade secrets have no time limitation. The agreement further provides that for a period of three years from December 30, YR-3, Paul will not solicit customers and employees of the business, and will use reasonable efforts to ensure that its representatives also do not.

Dynamo and Dillon claim that both before and after the closing of the sale of the business, Paul solicited two key employees, J.J. Lyons and Sal Duane, to work for her. Dillon contends that these employees were key to Dynamo's success and that this was in direct violation of their agreement. Within three months of the asset purchase, both employees began working for Sportique, Paul's new company. Dynamo and Dillon also accuse Paul of directing Lyons to take a valuable customer list that Paul had sold to Dillon and Dynamo as a trade secret. Dynamo and Dillon state that they first suspected the taking of the list in the late spring or early summer of YR-2, when their sales dropped, and customers they contacted had been contacted by J.J. Lyons. Dillon claims that he did not know for certain that Lyons had taken the list until Lyons was deposed. Hingle estimates that by the end of the second quarter of YR-2, 60 percent of the customers on the list had been contacted by Sportique, resulting in a significant loss of sales and revenue from the use of the list by Paul.

Paul alleges that Dynamo and Dillon fraudulently induced her to enter into the contract by presenting her with a false financial statement, and that such action makes the contract voidable. She denies solicitation of employees and denies asking Lyons to take the customer list. Further, she claims that Dillon breached the contract by failing to make the balloon payment in September, and cannot therefore enforce the contract terms now.

B. The Law

Preliminary Injunction Standards

A preliminary injunction is "an extraordinary remedy involving the exercise of a very far-reaching power, which is to be applied 'only in [the] limited circumstances which clearly demand it.'" *Direx Israel, Ltd. v. Breakthrough Medical Corp.*, 952 F.2d 802, 811 (4th Cir. 1991) (citations omitted). The sole purpose of a preliminary injunction is to preserve the status quo pending a full trial on the merits. A preliminary injunction is never awarded as a matter of right but is left to the sound discretion of the trial court. A court's discretion, however, does not replace a careful analysis of the four factors required for a preliminary injunction. *Winter v. Natural Resources Defense Council, Inc.*, 129 S.Ct. 365, 374 (2008). A court must make a fact-intensive analysis in each case to determine if injunctive relief is appropriate. To obtain a preliminary injunction, the party seeking injunctive relief must establish that:

1) he is likely to succeed on the merits;

2) he is likely to suffer irreparable harm in the absence of preliminary relief;

3) the balance of equities tips in his favor; and

4) an injunction is in the public interest.

The burden of establishing the four factors remains with the movant. The movant must establish a clear showing that the four factors have been met. This "clear showing" requires factual support beyond the allegations of the complaint, but the evidence need not strictly comply with the Federal Rules of Evidence. *Flynt Distributing Co. v. Harvey*, 734 F.2d 1389, 1394 (9th Cir. 1984).

1. Likelihood of Success on the Merits

a. The Trade Secrets Case

To prevail on their motion for a preliminary injunction, Dillon and Dynamo must show a likelihood of success on the merits of their case. Accordingly, they must argue that Paul breached their agreement by using the customer lists he purchased from Paul and that the list is a protected trade secret. The Uniform Trade Secrets Act, which has been adopted by Nita, defines a trade secret as:

> information, including a . . . compilation . . ., that:
>
> (i) derives independent economic value, actual or potential, from not being generally known to, and not being readily ascertainable by proper means by, other persons who can obtain economic value from its disclosure or use, and
>
> (ii) is the subject of efforts that are reasonable under the circumstances to maintain its secrecy.

Many courts, including Nita, have expanded the UTSA into a six-part test with the movant bearing the burden of proving each element:

"When determining whether information constitutes a trade secret (under Nita law), courts consider:

(1) the extent to which the information is known outside of the business;

(2) the extent to which it is known by employees and others involved in the business;

(3) the extent of measures taken by the business to guard the secrecy of the information;

(4) the value of the information to the business and its competitors;

(5) the amount of effort or money expended by the business in developing the information; and

(6) the ease or difficulty with which the information could be properly acquired or duplicated by others.

CDS., Inc. v. Zetler, 198 F. Supp. 3d 323 (S.D.N.Y. 2016) See also *Ultraflo v. Pelican Tank Parts, Inc.*, 926 F. Supp. 2d 935 (S.D. Tex. 2013); *178 Lowell Street Operating Co. v. Nichols*, 152 F. Supp. 3d 47 (D. Mass 2016) (preliminary injunction to stop the defendant from using customer lists).

"A trade secret is any formula, pattern, device or compilation which is used in one's business, and which gives the owner an opportunity to obtain an advantage over competitors who do not know or use it." *North Atlantic Instruments, Inc. v. Haber*, 188 F.3d 38, 44 (2d Cir. 1999) (citations omitted). Where a customer list is compiled through substantial effort and kept in confidence, it may be treated as a trade secret, provided the information contained therein is not otherwise readily available. *Id.*

In determining whether a list is a trade secret, one of the factors courts look to is efforts made by the owner to keep the list secret. Examples of measures the courts have examined in determining whether protections are reasonable are the use of employment and confidentiality agreements, computer password protection, alarm systems, and the installation of firewalls and security software. *Paz Systems, Inc. v. The Dakota Group Corp.*, 514 F. Supp. 2d 402 (E.D.N.Y. 2007). The determination of whether a customer list is a trade secret is a question of fact.

b. Fraudulent Inducement

Paul may argue that Dillon and Dynamo cannot show a likelihood of success on the merits because their agreement was fraudulently induced and therefore voidable.

To prove fraudulent inducement under Nita law, the plaintiff must establish by clear and convincing evidence 1) a material misrepresentation of a present existing or past fact; 2) an intent to deceive; 3) plaintiff's reasonable reliance on the misrepresentation; and 4) resulting damages.

A voidable contract is where one party may elect to either affirm the contract, avoiding the legal duties imposed by it, or to ratify the agreement, mandating performance of the contractual obligation by both parties. Restatement (Second) of Contracts § 7 (Supp. 2017). A typical instance of a voidable contract is one induced by fraud. *Id* at cmt. b.

2. Irreparable Harm

The threatened harm must be more than a possibility and it must be imminent. *Winter*, 129 S.Ct at 375. A preliminary injunction cannot be based on situations "where the harm is admittedly not present or immediate but merely problematic, conditioned on possible future events." *Direx Israel*, 952 F.2d at 816. More than a mere suspicion or only a remote risk of irreparable harm must be demonstrated. An injunction should not be granted "to eliminate a possibility of a remote future injury." *Acierno v. New Castle Cty.*, 40 F.3d. 645, 655 (3d Cir.1994). "There must be a substantial threat of impending injury before an injunction will issue." *Allis-Chalmers Manufacturing Co. v. Continental Aviation and Engineering Corp.*, 255 F. Supp. 645, 654 (E.D. Mich. 1966).

Irreparable injury means injury for which a monetary award cannot be adequate compensation. Generally, where money damages are adequate compensation a preliminary injunction will not issue. *Jackson Dairy, Inc. v. H.P. Hood & Sons, Inc.*, 596 F.2d 70, 72 (2d Cir. 1979). However, irreparable harm may still exist where the moving party's business cannot survive absent a preliminary injunction or where "[d]amages may be unobtainable because the respondent may become insolvent before a final judgment can be entered and collected." *Roland Mach. Co. v. Dresser Indus., Inc.*, 749 F.2d 380, 386 (7th Cir. 1984).

Preliminary injunctions are generally granted under the theory that there is an urgent need for speedy action to protect the rights of the movant. Delay in seeking enforcement of those rights, however, tends to indicate at least a reduced need for such drastic, speedy action. *Citybank, N.A. v Citytrust*, 756 F.2d 273, 275–76 (2d Cir. 1985).

3. Balance of the Equities

The court must weigh the respective hardships to the parties, and the balance of the harms must tip toward the movant. Both parties claim harm from either the issuance or failure to issue the requested relief. The court must determine the greater harm and the relative harm to each.

4. Public Interest

The movant must show that the injunction serves the public interest. Trade-secret disputes inevitably raise competing public interests and policies. On one side is the public policy in favor of permitting fair rewards for those who develop new methods, procedures, or technologies, which help provide incentives for innovation and progress. This policy favors awarding some form of monopoly protection for those who develop trade secrets. On the other side is a policy favoring free competition in the marketplace, which cuts against creating monopoly protections for trade secrets. *See Direx Israel*, 952 F.2d. Public interest is also implicated where the issuance of a preliminary injunction affects nonparties.

5. The Sliding Scale

Should the court find that Dillon and Dynamo have not met the traditional requirement of likelihood of success on the merits, the inquiry does not end. Nita, like many other jurisdictions, has adopted a "sliding scale" test. This test allows the court to weigh the balance of potential harms on a "sliding scale" against the movant's likelihood of success. The greater the balance of harms, the less the likelihood of success must weigh in the movant's favor. *Girl Scouts of Manitou Council v. Girl Scouts of United States of Am.*, 549 F.3d 1079, 1086 (7th Cir. 2008).

Nita's sliding-scale test survives *Winter*. As various federal circuits have held, Nita's circuit agrees with Justice Ginsburg's assessment in *Winter* that the "Court has never rejected [the sliding-scale] formulation, and I do not believe it does so today." *Winter*, 129 S.Ct. at 392 (Ginsburg, J., dissenting).

As Justice Ginsburg noted in *Winter*, "[f]lexibility is the hallmark of equity jurisdiction." *Id.* at 391. Preliminary injunctive relief protects the movant from irreparable harm and preserves the court's ability to render meaningful opinions after a full trial on the merits. In complex factual situations, where discovery is limited and speed is of the essence, flexibility and discretion are needed to preserve the court's power to order equitable relief.

The sliding-scale test allows the flexibility needed for injunctive relief. The test softens the likelihood-of-success prong to allow for injunctive relief where the likelihood of success is such that "serious questions" going to the merits were raised and the balance of the hardships tips sharply in the movant's favor, provided the other two prongs required for injunctive relief are met. *Alliance for the Wild Rockies v. Cottrell*, 632 F.3d 1127 (9th Cir. 2011).

Serious questions require more than a possibility of success on the merits. *See Winter* at 375. For the purposes of injunctive relief, serious questions "need not promise a certainty of success, nor even present a probability of success, but must involve a fair chance of success on the merits." *The Republic of the Phillipines v. Marcos*, 862 F.2d 1355, 1362 (9th Cir. 1988).

6. Scope of Injunctive Relief

The party whose behavior is to be enjoined must be able to understand from the order itself precisely what can and cannot be done. Because disobedience of an order can be punishable with contempt, Rule 65(d) demands that "[e]very order granting an injunction . . . shall be specific in terms; [and] shall describe in reasonable detail . . . the act or acts sought to be restrained . . . ." Fed. R. Civ. P. 65(d).

"An ordinary person reading the court's order should be able to ascertain from the document itself exactly what conduct is proscribed." *American Red Cross v. Palm Beach Blood Bank, Inc.*, 143 F.3d 1407, 1411 (11th Cir. 1998) (citations omitted). Even if the party receiving injunctive relief assures the court that it will not enforce the injunction in an inappropriate manner, a party enjoined "should not have to risk citation for contempt in order to determine the true scope of activity barred by the district court's order." *Id.* at 1412.

If injunctive relief is granted by the court, Dillon and Dynamo must post security in an amount that the court considers proper to pay the costs and damages sustained by Paul as a result of a wrongfully issued injunction. Fed. R. Civ. P. 65(c).

III. POSSIBLE ARGUMENTS FOR DILLON

A. Likelihood of Success on the Merits (Alternatively, serious questions going to the merits)

1. Customer List Qualifies as a Trade Secret Under the Uniform Trade Secret Act

The customer list qualifies as a trade secret under the requirements of the Uniform Trade Secrets Act.

a. UTSA Non-Secrecy Factors

The customer list contained information that was not readily known or ascertainable, and thus could not be duplicated without difficulty. The author of this list, Michelle Paul, created the initial list while in her job at Womensport by calling her personal contacts in the industry. These personal contacts provided the basis of the list, supplemented by public information such as trade journals and Google. The list includes not only high-end retail outlets in North America and the Caribbean, which admittedly could be identified through public sources, but also businesses in obscure locations that most companies would never identify, much less target. The list contains information about the people who ran each business, each business's history, and demographic information about the customers in each business's market locale. Client contacts fall within the scope of protectable trade secrets, as do individual customer preferences. *North Atlantic Instruments v. Haber*, 188 F.3d 38 (2d Cir. 1999.) Additionally, the Restatement of Law (Third) § 39, comment f, states that the secrecy of the list as a whole that is determinative. The fact that some of the components may be known does not preclude protection for the combination of the different elements.

Paul acknowledged in her deposition that she considered the customer list a valuable asset because it gave her an advantage over her competitors and that everyone knew it. She promoted the list as a valuable asset when she was looking for a buyer for Sportslifeware. Dillon was aware that the information contained in the list would give him a competitive advantage over others in the industry. The parties included "specialized customer list" in the terms of the asset purchase agreement, reflecting the parties' understanding of its value.

The value of the list is made apparent by Paul's own use of it when the list was brought by J.J. Lyons to Paul's new company. Paul testified that when she developed the list initially at her job at Womensport, she had the time to create the list. At Sportslifeware, she and Lyons worked on the list continually. Lyons testified that about 30 percent of his time at Sportslifeware may have been spent on the list, continuing to build and update it. But both Paul and Lyons testified that at Sportique they had little time to reconstruct the list. The level of detail contained on the list, and the time and effort that went into its construction and maintenance, demonstrate the difficulty in duplicating it.

Additionally, the value of the list is demonstrated by the immediate increase in sales at Sportique when Paul began using the list. Sportique was losing money during its initial months. Within weeks of Paul and Lyons adopting the list, orders were coming in from Sportslifeware's old customers, and within three or four months, Paul had gotten orders from almost 60 percent of customers from the list.

Even if all of the information on the list could arguably be duplicated by Paul and her employees from public sources over time, the fact remains that it was not. See *North Atlantic v. Haber, supra*, 188 F.3d at 46 ("[R]egardless of whether Apex *could* generate the list on its own, it did not").

b. UTSA Secrecy Factors

As to Dillon's measures to guard the secrecy of the information, the Uniform Trade Secrets Act requires a trade secret to be "the subject of efforts that are reasonable under the circumstances to maintain its secrecy." Under both Dillon and Paul, only the sales and marketing team had access to the list, and were directed never to show the list to anyone outside the team unless strictly necessary. Computers at Sportslifeware under both Dillon and Paul were password protected. Dillon did not have employees sign an employment agreement with a confidentiality requirement, as Paul did. But Dillon repeatedly told Sportslifeware employees they had to be careful with the list and keep it secret. J.J. Lyons and Pat Hingle both testified in their depositions that they knew it was important to keep the list confidential, with or without a written agreement. The Restatement of Law (Third) § 39, comment (g) states: "[I]f the value and secrecy of the information are clear, evidence of the specific precautions taken by the trade secret owner may be unnecessary." Here, Lyons and Hingle testified that they knew the value that Dillion placed on the customer list as an asset of Sportslifeware and that it was important to keep the list confidential. Significantly, the only person known to have taken the customer list was J.J. Lyons. The circumstances here are not comparable, for example, to the public release of secret customer information as in *American Red Cross*, 143 F.3d 1407, where confidential donor names were posted on a computer billboard.

2. Paul's Argument that the Asset Purchase Agreement is Voidable

Both Arthur Dillon and Michelle Paul acknowledged the customer list as a trade secret that Paul agreed to sell to Dillon. Paragraph 5.04(a) in the Asset Purchase Agreement defines trade secrets as including "specialized customer list." This list is the only asset that meets that definition. In fact, Paul marketed the customer list as an important and valuable asset of the company when selling it.

Any claim by Paul that the Asset Purchase Agreement was fraudulently induced and therefore voidable based on misrepresentation of his net worth is meritless. As Dillon testified in his deposition, his net worth at the time of closing in YR-3 in fact exceeded $13 million. Dillon testified that while the financial statement he submitted at closing did not reflect some loans he had taken out to meet obligations of Dynamo, other property had increased in value. Based on comparable property values, he believed his Arizona vacation home to be over $2.85 million at the time of closing, and the loan he had taken on that property had been reduced. He also testified that his New York residence had increased greatly in value during the same period. Therefore, Paul will not be able to succeed on this claim because she cannot prove the necessary intent for fraud.

B. Irreparable Harm

Any further loss of Sportslifeware's customers is the loss of the business itself. By late summer YR-2, the cash flow from Sportslifeware that Dillon counted on had been cut in half, with almost all lost customers stolen by Paul. Dynamo and Dillon face a substantial threat of irreparable injury by Paul's continued use of the customer list, resulting in the loss to Dynamo of customers and goodwill. The harm is imminent. Losing additional clients to Paul could bring an end to Sportslifeware, will drive Dynamo into bankruptcy, and may also result in financial ruin of its only stockholder. As noted in the Memorandum of Law, courts have held that irreparable harm may still exist where the moving party's business cannot survive absent preliminary injunction or where damages may become unobtainable because the party seeking injunction may become insolvent before a final judgment can be entered and collected.

Equitable relief is particularly appropriate in trade secrets cases because "loss of trade secrets cannot be measured in money damages" and therefore "[a] trade secret once lost is . . . lost forever." *North Atlantic Instruments, Inc. v. Haber, supra*, 188 F.3d 38, at p. 49. Moreover, Dillon seeks the preservation of his family business, not money damages. Dillon has been in the business of manufacturing and selling sporting and outdoor goods most of his life. His father started the business and Dillon has continued building the legacy. He wants to maintain it and continue to build it.

Dillon must anticipate that he will have to account for the delay in seeking injunctive relief. There are several possible arguments. The press of his failing business kept him from pursuing costly litigation, and he will demonstrate at trial that the failure of his business was directly caused by the theft of the customer list. Additionally, no action could be pursued effectively by Dillon until discovery was obtained. It was only through discovery that Dillon knew with certainty that Lyons had taken the list, and was using it at Paul's new business.

An allegation by Paul of unclean hands should not defeat this motion. Paul misappropriated the customer list before she came to believe that Dillon was worth less than $13 million, and well before Dillon was unable to make the balloon payment in September YR-2. Dillon asserts that he would have been able to make the balloon payment to Paul had she not misappropriated the list because Sportslifeware's sales would have covered that amount. Thus, Dillon's financial statements would have been irrelevant in the absence of Paul's taking of the customer list.

C. Balance of Harms

Because Dillon faces the imminent threat of the loss of his company, the balance of harms weighs in his favor. The injury caused by Paul's taking of the customer list outweighs any injury to Paul's new company. Any injuries incurred as a result of the alleged fraudulent inducement by Dillon or the failure to pay the balloon payment can be addressed by remedies in the trial court.

In contrast, the harm to Dillon should the injunction be denied is severe, and money damages in a subsequent trial is an inadequate remedy

D. Public Interest

Public interest favors the enforcement of contracts and the protection of trade secrets. Although Paul developed the customer list, she sold that list to Dillon and Dynamo. Moreover, the public interest is served when unfair competition is restrained.

E. Sliding Scale Approach

Even if the court finds that Dillon has not shown the level of proof necessary for the traditional likelihood of success showing, Dillon has demonstrated serious questions on the merits. He has shown there is a fair chance he will succeed on the merits that the customer list is a trade secret under the Uniform Trade Secrets Act and as defined in the Asset Purchase Agreement. Dillon did not fraudulently induce Paul to enter into the Asset Purchase Agreement, in view of his net worth at the time the time the agreement was signed. The balance of harms sharply tips in his favor. Without injunctive relief, Dillon may lose his company by the time this matter goes to trial. Any injuries to Paul can be addressed by remedies in the trial court. As discussed in "Possible Arguments for Dillon" under the traditional preliminary injunction approach, Dillon can show likelihood of irreparable injury and that injunctive relief is in the public interest.

F.   The Scope of Injunctive Relief

Dynamo and Dillon must craft an injunction order that clearly tells Paul what she is prohibited from doing. Some considerations might be:

1) If Dillon seeks "an immediate return of the customer lists alleged to constitute trade secrets; AND an order enjoining Paul, her company, employees, and agents from using these trade secrets," then what will Dillon propose as to pending orders? What about profits from customer orders placed from the time Paul and Lyons used the list at Sportique through to the present? Should the order address customer information in the memories of Paul and Lyons?

2) If Dynamo and Dillon seek "an order enjoining Paul, her company, employees, and agents from soliciting Sportslifeware's customers," Dillon should be prepared to address the exact definition of "solicitation of customers." Must Sportique refuse a customer on the list who contacts Sportique?

3) If Dynamo and Dillon are seeking to enjoin Paul from soliciting and recruiting and hiring employees, what should the order say as to whether former employees can ever contact Paul and be hired? Does the order need to address Lyons' current employment with Paul? Finally, this particular prohibition has a three-year limitation, a limitation that will expire in December of this year. Dillon must ask the court to interpret the status quo as continuing that provision beyond the date stated in the contract. Dillon should expect that Paul will argue that this court of equity cannot give the defendant rights beyond those given in the contract, especially considering his delay in raising these issues for more than a year after his knowledge of them.

IV. Possible Arguments for Paul

A. Likelihood of Success on the Merits (Alternatively, serious questions going to the merits)

1. The Customer List is Not a Trade Secret

a. UTSA Non-Secrecy Factors

The customer list created by Ms. Paul is not a trade secret under the Uniform Trade Secrets Act. The origin of this list was information that was publicly sourced: names and addresses of customers. "If information is readily ascertainable from public sources such as trade directories or phone books, then customer lists will not be considered a trade secret. . . ." (*Ed Nowogroski Insurance Inc. v. Rucker*, 971 P.2d 936, 944 (1999). Both Paul and Lyons testified that they could have duplicated the list, given the time and the resources. The list here is not like the formula for Coke or other intellectual property. It is a collection of accessible customer information. While the list took Ms. Paul nearly a year to develop, it could be replicated through hard work.

b. UTSA Secrecy Factors

Finally, even assuming that the customer list was a trade secret at the time of purchase, Dillon failed to take reasonable efforts to maintain the secrecy of the information contained in that customer list, and the list lost its status as a trade secret.

In contrast to Paul, Dillon did not require his employees to sign an employee agreement with a confidentiality provision. Dillon did not implement other policies used at Sportique to ensure the secrecy of the list. At Sportique, J.J. Lyons monitored who had the list, and that it was used only a need-to-know basis. Lyons had members of the sales team "sign out" the list when they took the list home to work. Pat Hingle testified that under Dillon, he was unsure who had responsibility for ensuring the secrecy of the list. Controls were lax. There was no system for tracking who had the list to ensure its secrecy. In the office, there were printed copies of the customer list and copies of the list on thumb drives.

2. The Asset Purchase Agreement is Voidable

At the outset, Paul can argue that the contract was fraudulently induced based on Dillon's misrepresentations on his financial statements. When the Memorandum of Agreement was signed on March 24, YR-3, defendant Dillon provided Paul with a personal financial statement that purported to demonstrate a financial net worth of $13 million. In the Memorandum of Agreement, Dillon agreed to provide at the time of closing a current and accurate financial statement. Paul agreed to complete the purchase and sale only if Dillon's net worth at the time of closing was not less than $13 million. In her fraud in the inducement claim, Paul alleges that on December 23, YR-3, Dillon executed an inaccurate personal financial statement that failed to disclose that Dillon was worth less than $13 million for the purpose of inducing Paul to sell her business, Sportslifeware. Paul expressly relied upon the intentionally false and fraudulent statement to enter into the asset purchase agreement. As a result of this fraud, the contract is voidable. Paul can choose to disaffirm the Asset Purchase Agreement in its entirety. Paul must consider the consequences of asking for the contract to be rescinded.

B. Irreparable Harm

Dillon's lack of diligence in seeking a preliminary injunction defeats his claim of irreparable harm. Dillon's and Hingle's depositions demonstrate that as early as the second quarter of YR-2 they were suspicious that the customer list had been taken and was being used by Paul's new company. Dillon took no action during YR-2. In fact, Dillon never initiated any lawsuit based on the breach of contract or fraudulent inducement actions now claimed in the counterclaim. Those claims only appeared after he was sued by Paul in March of YR-1 for failing to make the $5.5 million payment in September YR-2, and can be seen as a defensive smokescreen. At least a year elapsed before Dillon alleged imminent harm from these actions.

Additionally, Dynamo does not face a threat of irreparable injury based on Paul's use of the customer list because it is Dillon's own years of mismanagement and poor decision making that created his situation. Hingle testified in his deposition that when Dillon took over Sportslifeware he seemed strapped for cash. It was believed that Dillon was draining all the income, including some needed for expenses, out of the company. Dillon seemed unwilling to put profits back into the operation of the business and to spend money for capital expenditures. The harm here was created by Dillon years ago and is continuing. It is not "immediate." Any losses caused by Paul's use of the customer list can be compensated by money damages. These are matters that should be resolved at trial.

C. Balance of Harms

Third-party customers have contracts with Paul that must be honored. If the injunction is granted, Paul's new business will be significantly damaged and customers injured if she is estopped from fulfilling orders. Paul may argue that it is likely she will go out of business if this injunction is granted. Since Dynamo and Dillon have not paid for the business or its assets, equity favors her. Dillon should not receive the benefit of a deal he has not paid for.

D. Public Interest

Public interest favors free competition in the marketplace. Here, even if the customer list is determined to be a trade secret, the effect of an injunction upon the customers who have pending orders or the preference to place future orders with Sportique must be considered by the court. Additionally, while public interest favors enforcement of a contract, such an interest is not served when the contract was induced by fraud.

E. Sliding Scale Argument

Nor should a preliminary injunction issue under the alternate sliding scale approach. Dillon cannot show serious questions going to the merits because the customer list does not qualify as a trade secret under the Uniform Trade Secrets Act and Dillon fraudulently induced Paul to enter into the asset purchase agreement that defines a customer list as a trade secret. The balance of harms does not tip sharply in Dillon's favor. The loss of Dillon's business is attributed in large part to his own mismanagement. Paul's business will be significantly damaged and the interests of third parties who are in contract with Paul will be injured if an injunction is issued. As discussed in the "Possible Arguments for Paul" under the traditional preliminary injunction approach, money damages can compensate Dillon, thus countering Dillon's irreparable injury argument. The public interest is served by denying the preliminary injunction.

F. Scope of the Injunction

The issues that Paul will raise about the scope of any injunctive relief depend upon how Dillon addresses the problems outlined in his possible argument, above. Some considerations might be:

1) If Dillon is granted an injunction, Paul will seek an order that is not only narrow, but informs with specificity what she can and cannot do. Paul may argue that even the most carefully crafted order may require extensive court supervision pending trial, an outcome the court would not favor.

2) If Dynamo and Dillon seeks "an immediate return of the customer lists alleged to constitute trade secrets; and an order enjoining Paul, her company, employees, and agents from using these trade secrets," what do Dynamo and Dillon want to include in the order about pending orders, and customers who call Sportique with repeat orders and other issues? How should the preliminary injunction order address Paul's profits from customer orders placed from the time Paul and Lyons used the list at Sportique through to the present? Should the order address customer information in the memories of Paul and Lyons?

3) If Dynamo and Dillon seek "an order enjoining Paul, her company, employees, and agents from soliciting Sportslifeware's customers, how should "solicitation" be defined? Must Sportique refuse a sale to a customer from the list who contacts them?

4) If Dynamo and Dillon are seeking to enjoin Paul from hiring Sportslifeware employees, how will "solicitation" be defined? Can Paul ever hire a former employee who approaches Sportique for employment? Finally, this particular prohibition has a three-year limitation, a limitation that will expire in December of this year. Dillon will probably ask the court to interpret the status quo as continuing that provision beyond the date stated in the contract. Paul may argue that this court of equity cannot give the defendant rights beyond those given in the contract, especially considering his delay in raising these issues for more than a year after his knowledge of them.

V. Uniform Trade Secrets Act and the Restatement, Rule 65

A. Uniform Trade Secrets Act

Section 1. Definitions

As used in this Act, unless the context requires otherwise:

* * *

(4) "Trade Secret" means information, including a formula, pattern, compilation, program, device, method, technique, or process, that:

    (i) derives independent economic value, actual or potential, from not being generally known to, and not being readily ascertainable by proper means by, other persons who can obtain economic value from its disclosure or use, and

    (ii) is the subject of efforts that are reasonable under the circumstances to maintain its secrecy.

B. Restatement of the Law (Third), Unfair Competition, Section 39

Chapter 4. Appropriation of Trade Values

Topic 2. Trade Secrets

Section 39. DEFINITION OF TRADE SECRET

A trade secret is any information that can be used in the operation of a business or other enterprise and that is sufficiently valuable and secret to afford an actual or potential economic advantage over others.

Comment:

* * *

d. Subject matter. A trade secret can consist of a formula, pattern, compilation of data, computer program, device, method, technique, process, or other form or embodiment of economically valuable information. . . . A trade secret can also relate to . . . the identity and requirements of customers (see § 42, Comment f).

An agreement between the parties that characterizes specific information as a "trade secret" can be an important although not necessarily conclusive factor in determining whether the information qualifies for protection as a trade secret under this Section. As a precaution against disclosure, such an agreement is evidence of the value and secrecy of the information, and can also supply or contribute to the definiteness required in delineating the trade secret. The agreement can also be important in establishing a duty of confidence. However, because of the public interest in preserving access to information that is in the public domain, such an agreement will not ordinarily stop a defendant from contesting the existence of a trade secret.

It is not possible to state precise criteria for determining the existence of a trade secret. The status of information claimed as a trade secret must be ascertained through a comparative evaluation of all the relevant factors, including the value, secrecy, and definiteness of the information as well as the nature of the defendant's misconduct.

e. Requirement of value. A trade secret must be of sufficient value in the operation of a business or other enterprise to provide an actual or potential economic advantage over others who do not possess the information. The advantage, however, need not be great.

f. Requirement of secrecy. To qualify as a trade secret, the information must be secret. The secrecy, however, need not be absolute. The rule stated in this Section requires only secrecy sufficient to confer an actual or potential economic advantage on one who possesses the information. Thus, the requirement of secrecy is satisfied if it would be difficult or costly for others who could exploit the information to acquire it without resort to wrongful conduct. . . .

Information that is generally known or readily ascertainable through proper means by others to whom it has potential economic value is not protectable as a trade secret. . . . However, it is the secrecy of the claimed trade secret as a whole that is determinative. The fact that some or all of the components of the trade secret are well-known does not preclude protection for a secret combination, compilation, or integration of the individual elements.

* * *

Circumstantial evidence is admissible to establish that information is not readily ascertainable through proper means and hence is eligible for protection as a trade secret. Precautions taken by the claimant to preserve the secrecy of the information, the precautions taken by the plaintiff to protect the secrecy of the information, and the willingness of others to pay for access to the information.

The plaintiff's use of the trade secret in the operation of its business is itself some evidence of the information's value. Identifiable benefits realized by the trade secret owner through use of the information are also evidence of value. . . .

g. Precautions to maintain secrecy. Precautions taken to maintain the secrecy of information are relevant in determining whether the information qualifies for protection as a trade secret. Precautions to maintain secrecy may take many forms, including physical security designed to prevent unauthorized access, procedures intended to limit disclosure based upon the "need to know," and measures that emphasize to recipients the confidential nature of the information such as nondisclosure agreements, signs, and restrictive legends. Such precautions can be evidence of the information's value and secrecy.

The Uniform Trade Secrets Act requires a trade secret to be "the subject of efforts that are reasonable under the circumstances to maintain its secrecy." . . . Whether viewed as an independent requirement or as an element to be considered with other factors relevant to the existence of a trade secret, the owner's precautions should be evaluated in light of the other available evidence relating to the value and secrecy of the information. Thus, if the value and secrecy of the information are clear, evidence of specific precautions taken by the trade secret owner may be unnecessary.

The precautions taken by the trade secret owner are also relevant to other potential issues in an action for the appropriation of a trade secret. They can signal to employees and other recipients that a disclosure of the information by the trade secret owner is intended to be in confidence. . . . They can also be relevant in determining whether a defendant possessed the knowledge necessary for the imposition of liability . . . and whether an accidental disclosure results in the loss of trade secret rights. . . .

§ 41 DUTY OF CONFIDENCE

A person to whom a trade secret has been disclosed owes a duty of confidence to the owner of the trade secret for purposes of the rule stated in § 40 if:

(a) the person made an express promise of confidentiality prior to the disclosure of the trade secret; or

(b) the trade secret was disclosed to the person under circumstances in which the relationship between the parties to the disclosure or the other facts surrounding the disclosure justify the conclusions that, at the time of the disclosure,

(1) the person knew or had reason to know that the disclosure was intended to be in confidence, and

(2) the other party to the disclosure was reasonable in inferring that the person consented to an obligation of confidentiality.

C. Federal Rules of Civil Procedure

Rule 65. Injunctions and Restraining Orders

(a) Preliminary Injunction.

* * *

(c) Security. The court may issue a preliminary injunction or a temporary restraining order only if the movant gives security in an amount that the court considers proper to pay the costs and damages sustained by any party found to have been wrongfully enjoined or restrained. The United States, its officers, and its agencies are not required to give security.

(d) Contents and Scope of Every Injunction and Restraining Order.

(1) *Contents.* Every order granting an injunction and every restraining order must:

(A) state the reasons why it issued;

(B) state its terms specifically; and

(C) describe in reasonable detail—and not by referring to the complaint or other document—the act or acts restrained or required.

VI. CASE LAW

A. *Winter v. Natural Resources Defense Council, Inc.,* 555 U.S. 7 (2008)

Justice Breyer, with whom Justice Stevens joined as to Part I, concurred in part and dissented in part, and filed opinion.

Justice Ginsburg, with whom Justice Souter joined, dissented and filed opinion.

Opinion

Chief Justice ROBERTS delivered the opinion of the Court.

"To be prepared for war is one of the most effectual means of preserving peace." 1 Messages and Papers of the President's 57 (J. Richardson comp. 1897). So said George Washington in his first Annual Address to Congress, 218 years ago. One of the most important ways the Navy prepares for war is through integrated training exercises at sea. . . . The Court of Appeals upheld a preliminary injunction imposing restrictions on the Navy's sonar training, even though that court acknowledged that "the record contains no evidence that marine mammals have been harmed" by the Navy's exercises. 518 F.3d 658, 696 (C.A.9 2008). The Court of Appeals was wrong, and its decision is reversed.

A plaintiff seeking a **preliminary injunction** must establish that he is likely to succeed on the merits, that he is likely to suffer irreparable harm in the absence of preliminary relief, that the balance of equities tips in his favor, and that an injunction is in the **public** interest. See *Munaf v. Geren,* 553 U.S. 674, 689–690, 128 S.Ct. 2207, 2218–2219, 171 L.Ed.2d 1 (2008); *Amoco Production Co. v. Gambell,* 480 U.S. 531, 542, 107 S.Ct. 1396, 94 L.Ed.2d 542 (1987); *Weinberger v. Romero–Barcelo,* 456 U.S. 305, 311–312, 102 S.Ct. 1798, 72 L.Ed.2d 91 (1982).

The District Court and the Ninth Circuit concluded that plaintiffs have shown a likelihood of success on the merits of their National Environmental Policy Act claim. The Navy strongly disputes this determination. . . .

The District Court and the Ninth Circuit also held that when a plaintiff demonstrates a strong likelihood of prevailing on the merits, a **preliminary injunction** may be entered based only on a "possibility" of irreparable harm. (citations omitted) The lower courts held that plaintiffs had met this standard because the scientific studies, declarations, and other evidence in the record established to "a near certainty" that the Navy's training exercises would cause irreparable harm to the environment. (citations omitted)

The Navy challenges these holdings, arguing that plaintiffs must demonstrate a likelihood of irreparable injury—not just a possibility—in order to obtain preliminary relief. . . .

We agree with the Navy that the Ninth Circuit's "possibility" standard is too lenient. Our frequently reiterated standard requires plaintiffs seeking preliminary relief to demonstrate that irreparable injury is *likely* in the absence of an injunction. . . . (citations omitted)

Issuing a **preliminary injunction** based only on a possibility of irreparable harm is inconsistent with our characterization of injunctive relief as an extraordinary remedy that may only be awarded upon a clear showing that the plaintiff is entitled to such relief. *Mazurek v. Armstrong,* 520 U.S. 968, 972, 117 S.Ct. 1865, 138 L.Ed.2d 162 (1997) (*per curiam*).

* * *

A **preliminary injunction** is an extraordinary remedy never awarded as of right. *Munaf,* 553 U.S., at 689–690, 128 S.Ct., at 2218–2219. In each case, courts "must balance the competing claims of injury and must consider the effect on each party of the granting or withholding of the requested relief." *Amoco Production Co.,* 480 U.S., at 542, 107 S.Ct. 1396. "In exercising their sound discretion, courts of equity should pay particular regard for the public consequences in employing the extraordinary remedy of injunction." *Romero–Barcelo,* 456 U.S., at 312, 102 S.Ct. 1798; see also *Railroad Comm'n of Tex. v. Pullman Co.,* 312 U.S. 496, 500, 61 S.Ct. 643, 85 L.Ed. 971 (1941). In this case, the District Court and the Ninth Circuit significantly understated the burden the **preliminary injunction** would impose on the Navy's ability to conduct realistic training exercises, and the injunction's consequent adverse impact on the **public** interest in national defense.

* * *

These interests must be weighed against the possible harm to the ecological, scientific, and recreational interests that are legitimately before this Court. Plaintiffs contend that the Navy's use of MFA sonar will injure marine mammals or alter their behavioral patterns, impairing plaintiffs' ability to study and observe the animals. While we do not question the seriousness of these interests, we conclude that the balance of equities and consideration of the overall **public** interest in this case tip strongly in favor of the Navy. . . .

The **public** interest in conducting training exercises with active sonar under realistic conditions plainly outweighs the interests advanced by the plaintiffs. Of course, military interests do not always trump other considerations, and we have not held that they do. In this case, however, the proper determination of where the **public** interest lies does not strike us as a close question.

Reversed.

Justice GINSBURG, with whom Justice SOUTER joins, dissenting

* * *

Flexibility is a hallmark of equity jurisdiction. "The essence of equity jurisdiction has been the power of the Chancellor to do equity and to mould each decree to the necessities of the particular case. Flexibility rather than rigidity has distinguished it." *Weinberger v. Romero–Barcelo,* 456 U.S. 305, 312, 102 S.Ct. 1798, 72 L.Ed.2d 91 (1982) (quoting *Hecht Co. v. Bowles,* 321 U.S. 321, 329, 64 S.Ct. 587, 88 L.Ed. 754 (1944)). Consistent with equity's character, courts do not insist that litigants uniformly show a particular, predetermined quantum of probable success or injury before awarding equitable relief. Instead, courts have evaluated claims for equitable relief on a "sliding scale," sometimes awarding relief based on a lower likelihood of harm when the likelihood of success is very high. 11A C. Wright, A. Miller, & M. Kane, Federal Practice and Procedure § 2948.3, p. 195 (2d ed.1995). This Court has never rejected that formulation, and I do not believe it does so today.

Equity's flexibility is important in the National Environmental Policy Act context. Because an environmental impact statement is the tool for *uncovering* environmental harm, environmental plaintiffs may often rely more heavily on their probability of success than the likelihood of harm. The Court is correct that relief is not warranted "simply to prevent the possibility of some remote future injury." *52 *Ante,* at 375 (quoting Wright & Miller, *supra,* § 2948.1, at 155). "However, the injury need not have been inflicted when application is made or be certain to occur; a strong threat of irreparable injury before trial is an adequate basis." Wright & Miller, *supra,* § 2948.1, at 155–156 (footnote omitted). I agree with the District Court that Natural Resources Defense Council made the required showing here.

* * *

For the reasons stated, I would affirm the judgment of the Ninth Circuit.

B. *Alliance for the Wild Rockies v. Cottrell,* 632 F.3d 1127 (9th Cir. 2011)

W. FLETCHER, Circuit Judge:

Alliance for the Wild Rockies ("AWR") appeals the district court's denial of its motion for a preliminary injunction. AWR seeks to enjoin a timber salvage sale proposed by the United States Forest Service. Citing *Winter v. Natural Resources Defense Council,* 555 U.S. 7, 129 S.Ct. 365, 172 L.Ed.2d 249 (2008), the district court held that AWR had not shown the requisite likelihood of irreparable injury and success on the merits.

* * *

I. Background

In August and September of 2007, the Rat Creek Wildfire burned about 27,000 acres in the Beaverhead–Deerlodge National Forest in Montana. On July 1, 2009, almost two years later, the Chief Forester of the Forest Service made an Emergency Situation Determination for the Rat Creek Salvage Project ("the Project"). The Emergency Situation Determination permitted the immediate commencement of the Project's logging without any of the delays that might have resulted from the Forest Service's administrative appeals process.

The Project permits salvage logging of trees on approximately 1,652 of the 27,000 acres that were burned. The logging will take place (and to some degree has already taken place) on thirty-five units of land ranging from 3 to 320 acres in size.

* * *

On June 15, 2009, the Acting Forest Supervisor for the Beaverhead–Deerlodge National Forest wrote to the Regional Forester requesting that the Chief Forester make an Emergency Situation Determination ("ESD") in connection with the Rat Creek Project.

* * *

On July 1, 2009, the Chief Forester granted the request for an ESD.

* * *

Plaintiff AWR filed suit in federal district court alleging violations of the Appeals Reform Act ("ARA"), the National Forest Management Act ("NFMA"), and the National Environmental Protection Act ("NEPA"). In a brief order entered on August 14, 2009, the district court denied AWR's request for a preliminary injunction. After quoting *Winter,* the court wrote, "After reviewing the parties' filings, the Court is convinced Plaintiffs do not show a likelihood of success on the merits, nor that irreparable injury is likely in the absence of an injunction. This determination prevents the issuance of a preliminary injunction at this stage of the proceedings." The court did not describe or analyze the merits of AWR's claims and did not describe or analyze the harm alleged by AWR. The court denied AWR's motion for a stay and injunction pending appeal to this court.

Barry Smith Logging began work on the Project on August 21, 2009. The parties indicated at oral argument that approximately 49% of the planned logging was completed before winter conditions halted operations.

AWR timely appealed the district court's denial of its request for a preliminary injunction. Because a significant amount of the Project remains to be completed, this appeal is not moot.

II. Standard of Review

We review a district court's denial of a preliminary injunction for abuse of discretion. *Lands Council v. McNair*, 537 F.3d 981, 986 (9th Cir. 2008) (en banc). An abuse of discretion will be found if the district court based its decision "on an erroneous legal standard or clearly erroneous finding of fact." *Id.* "We review conclusions of law de novo and findings of fact for clear error." *Id.* at 986–87. We will not reverse the district court where it "got the law right," even if we "would have arrived at a different result," so long as the district court did not clearly err in its factual determinations. *Id.* at 987 (internal citations omitted).

III. Discussion

A. "Sliding Scale" and "Serious Questions" after *Winter*

In *Winter*, the Supreme Court disagreed with one aspect of this circuit's approach to preliminary injunctions. We had held that the "possibility" of irreparable harm was sufficient, in some circumstances, to justify a preliminary injunction. *Winter* explicitly rejected that approach. *Winter*, 129 S.Ct. at 375–76. Under *Winter,* plaintiffs must establish that irreparable harm is likely, not just possible, in order to obtain a preliminary injunction. *Id.* The Court wrote, "A plaintiff seeking a preliminary injunction must establish that he is likely to succeed on the merits, that he is likely to suffer irreparable harm in the absence of preliminary relief, that the balance of equities tips in his favor, and that an injunction is in the public interest." *Id.* at 374. "A preliminary injunction is an extraordinary remedy never awarded as of right." *Id.* at 376.

The majority opinion in *Winter* did not, however, explicitly discuss the continuing validity of the "sliding scale" approach to preliminary injunctions employed by this circuit and others. Under this approach, the elements of the preliminary injunction test are balanced, so that a stronger showing of one element may offset a weaker showing of another. For example, a stronger showing of irreparable harm to plaintiff might offset a lesser showing of likelihood of success on the merits. *See, e.g., Clear Channel Outdoor, Inc. v. City of Los Angeles,* 340 F.3d 810, 813 (9th Cir. 2003). This circuit has adopted and applied a version of the sliding scale approach under which a preliminary injunction could issue where the likelihood of success is such that "serious questions going to the merits were raised and the balance of hardships tips sharply in [plaintiff's] favor." *Id.* That test was described in this circuit as one alternative on a continuum. *See, e.g., Lands Council,* 537 F.3d at 987. The test at issue here has often been referred to as the "serious questions" test. We will so refer to it as well.

The parties in this case have devoted substantial portions of their argument to the question of the continuing validity of the "serious questions" approach to preliminary injunctions after *Winter.* For the reasons that follow, we hold that the "serious questions" approach survives *Winter* when applied as part of the four-element *Winter* test. In other words, "serious questions going to the merits" and a hardship balance that tips sharply toward the plaintiff can support issuance of an injunction, assuming the other two elements of the *Winter* test are also met.

* * *

The Seventh Circuit was the first to hold that the sliding scale test survives *Winter*, and that a weaker claim on the merits can still justify a preliminary injunction depending on the amount of "net harm" that could be prevented by the injunction. Citing *Winter*, Judge Easterbrook wrote:

> Irreparable injury is not enough to support equitable relief. There also must be a plausible claim on the merits, and the injunction must do more good than harm (which is to say that the "balance of equities" favors the plaintiff). How strong a claim on the merits is enough depends on the balance of harms: the more net harm an injunction can prevent, the weaker the plaintiff's claim on the merits can be while still supporting some preliminary relief.

* * *

[T]he value of this circuit's approach to assessing the merits of a claim at the preliminary injunction stage lies in its flexibility in the face of varying factual scenarios and the greater uncertainties inherent at the outset of particularly complex litigation.

The Supreme Court's recent opinions . . . have not undermined its approval of the more flexible approach. . . . None of the three cases comments at all, much less negatively, upon the application of a preliminary injunction standard that softens a strict "likelihood" [of success] requirement in cases that warrant it.

* * *

If the Supreme Court had meant for *Munaf, Winter,* or *Nken* to abrogate the more flexible standard for a preliminary injunction, one would expect some reference to the considerable history of the flexible standards applied in this circuit, seven of our sister circuits, and in the Supreme Court itself. . . . We have found no command from the Supreme Court that would foreclose the application of our established "serious questions" standard as a means of assessing a movant's likelihood of success on the merits. . . . Thus, we hold that our venerable standard for assessing a movant's probability of success on the merits remains valid. . . .

* * *

It would be most unfortunate if the Supreme Court or the Ninth Circuit had eliminated the longstanding discretion of a district judge to preserve the *status quo* with provisional relief until the merits could be sorted out in cases where clear irreparable injury would otherwise result and at least "serious questions" going to the merits are raised. . . .

Can it possibly be that the Supreme Court and Ninth Circuit have taken away the ability of district judges to preserve the *status quo* pending at least some discovery and further hearing on the merits in such cases?

* * *

For the reasons identified by our sister circuits and our district courts, we . . . conclud[e} that the "serious questions" version of the sliding scale test for preliminary injunctions remains viable after the Supreme Court's decision in *Winter.* In this circuit, the test has been formulated as follows:

A preliminary injunction is appropriate when a plaintiff demonstrates . . . that serious questions going to the merits were raised and the balance of hardships tips sharply in the plaintiff's favor. *Lands Council,* 537 F.3d at 987 (internal quotations and modification omitted). Of course, plaintiffs must also satisfy the other *Winter* factors.

* * *

But the "serious questions" approach survives *Winter* when applied as part of the four-element *Winter* test. That is, "serious questions going to the merits" and a balance of hardships that tips sharply towards the plaintiff can support issuance of a preliminary injunction, so long as the plaintiff also shows that there is a likelihood of irreparable injury and that the injunction is in the public interest.

B. Preliminary Injunction

Because it did not apply the "serious questions" test, the district court made an error of law in denying the preliminary injunction sought by AWR. We conclude that AWR has shown that there is a likelihood of irreparable harm; that there are at least serious questions on the merits concerning the validity of the Forest Service's Emergency Situation Determination; that the balance of hardships tips sharply in its favor; and that the public interest favors a preliminary injunction.

1. Likelihood of Irreparable Harm

Winter tells us that plaintiffs may not obtain a preliminary injunction unless they can show that irreparable harm is likely to result in the absence of the injunction. AWR's members use the Beaverhead–Deerlodge National Forest, including the areas subject to logging under the Project, for work and recreational purposes, such as hunting, fishing, hiking, horseback riding, and cross-country skiing. AWR asserts that its members' interests will be irreparably harmed by the Rat Creek Project. In particular, AWR asserts that the Project will harm its members' ability to "view, experience, and utilize" the areas in their undisturbed state.

The Forest Service responds that the Project areas represent only six percent of the acreage damaged by fire. It argues that because AWR members can "view, experience, and utilize" other areas of the forest, including other fire-damaged areas that are not part of the Project, they are not harmed by logging in the Project.

This argument proves too much. Its logical extension is that a plaintiff can never suffer irreparable injury resulting from environmental harm in a forest area as long as there are other areas of the forest that are not harmed. The Project will prevent the use and enjoyment by AWR members of 1,652 acres of the forest. This is hardly a de minimus injury.

* * *

2. Likelihood of Success on the Merits

AWR's strongest argument on the merits is that the Forest Service has violated the Appeals Reform Act ("ARA") and its implementing regulations by granting the Emergency Situation Designation ("ESD"). Regulations promulgated under the ARA provide that most Forest Service decisions are appealable through an administrative process. *See* 36 C.F.R. § 215.1 *et seq.*; Forest Service Decisionmaking and Appeals Reform Act, Pub.L. No. 102–381, Title III, § 322, 106 Stat. 1374, 1419–21 (1992). The administrative appeals process would ordinarily be available for the Project at issue in this case. 36 C.F.R. § 215.11(a) (including as appealable decisions those for "projects and activities implementing land and resource management plans ... documented in a Record of Decision (ROD) or Decision Notice (DN)"). If the Forest Service decision had been appealed administratively, there would have been an opportunity for members of the public, including plaintiffs, to object to the Project on various grounds. Implementation would then have been delayed until at least "the 15th business day following the date of appeal disposition." 36 C.F.R. § 215.9(b).

The regulations provide an exception to the appeals process when the Forest Service makes an ESD. An ESD allows work to begin on a project as soon as notice of the otherwise appealable project decision is appropriately published. 36 C.F.R. § 215.10(c).

* * *

In granting the ESD for this Project, the Chief Forester considered three factors: (1) the loss of receipts to the government due to delayed commencement of the Project; (2) the potential loss of an "opportunity to accomplish Douglas-fir planting and dwarf mistletoe control objectives"; and (3) the "importance this project has to the local economy of southwest Montana." We hold that, at a minimum, there are "serious questions" on the merits whether these three factors are sufficient to justify the ESD. We consider in turn the three factors upon which the Chief Forester relied.

First, the potential loss of receipts to the government resulting from the delay inherent in the appeals process was not great. The Chief Forester wrote that a delay of the commencement of the project until the summer of 2010 would result in a "projected loss of receipts to the government of as much as $16,000." The Chief Forester wrote, in addition, that if the commencement of the project were delayed until 2010, this would "significantly increase[ ] the likelihood of receiving no bids." "An absence of bids would push the potential loss to the government to $70,000." With all due respect to the budgetary concerns of the Forest Service, a loss of anticipated revenues to the government of "as much as $16,000," or even a "potential loss" of $70,000 in the event of no bids, is likely not a "substantial loss . . . to the Federal Government."

Even if $70,000 might, in some contexts, constitute a "substantial loss," that figure here is highly speculative. The Chief Forester indicated that a one-year delay would "significantly increase[ ] the likelihood of receiving no bids," but we cannot know precisely what that statement means. We do know that with a 2009 commencement date, multiple bids were submitted almost immediately, and one was accepted. The likelihood of not receiving a bid in 2009 appears to have been essentially zero. An increase from a likelihood of essentially 0% to a likelihood of 10% would be a significant increase in likelihood. But a 10% risk of receiving no bids results in a risk-adjusted loss of 10% of $70,000, or $7,000. A risk-adjusted loss of $7,000 is not significant.

Second, the loss of the opportunity to "accomplish Douglas-fir planting and dwarf mistletoe objectives" would be an actual loss only if there were no successful bid on the Project. That is, the Chief Forester concluded that if there were a bid on the Project, the monetary loss to the government would be "as much as $16,000." But in that event, there would be no loss of opportunity to plant Douglas firs or to control dwarf mistletoe, for those objectives would be accomplished by means of the logging contract. Only if there were no bids on the contract would the opportunity be lost. For the reasons just discussed, the possibility of no bids appears to us to be highly speculative. In addition, the Forest Service did not even attempt to quantify the extent of its mistletoe abatement objectives that would be achieved through this Project. It is unclear from the record whether the acres selected are particularly infested with mistletoe and therefore the Project is essential to the Forest Service's goals, or if mistletoe abatement on these acres is simply a serendipitous byproduct of the Project.

Third, the Chief Forester took into account the importance of the Project to the local economy of southwest Montana. As discussed below, this factor is relevant to the public interest element of the preliminary injunction analysis. But the impact of a project on a local economy is not one of the factors the Chief Forester was permitted to consider in deciding whether to issue an ESD. Under Forest Service regulations, she was permitted to consider "hazards threatening human health and safety or natural resources" and any "substantial loss of economic value to the Federal Government." 36 C.F.R. § 215.2. Neither the regulation, nor the ARA, permits consideration of the local economy in making an ESD determination. Thus, in relying on the third factor, the Chief Forester "relied on factors Congress did not intend [her] to consider." *Lands Council,* 537 F.3d at 987.

Finally, we note that the Forest Service has not been able to make clear to us, either in its briefing or at oral argument, why it waited so long to request an ESD. The Rat Creek fire occurred in August and September of 2007. The ESD was requested, and then issued, almost two years later. The delay in requesting an ESD obviously undermines the Chief Forester's determination in July 2009 that there was an Emergency Situation that justified the elimination of otherwise available administrative appeals.

We therefore conclude that AWR has, at a minimum, raised "serious questions" on the merits of its claim regarding the validity of the Chief Forester's Emergency Situation Determination.

3. Balance of Hardships

We conclude that the balance of hardships between the parties tips sharply in favor of AWR. When the question was before the district court, logging was contemplated on 1,652 acres of land in the Beaverhead–Deerlodge National Forest. Once those acres are logged, the work and recreational opportunities that would otherwise be available on that land are irreparably lost.

In addition, AWR was harmed by its inability to participate in the administrative appeals process, and that harm is perpetuated by the Project's approval. The administrative appeals process would have allowed AWR to challenge the Project under both NFMA and NEPA, and to seek changes in the Project before final approval by the Forest Service. Such administrative appeals sometimes result in significant changes to proposed projects.

The hardship to the Forest Service, set against the hardship to AWR, is an estimated potential foregone revenue of "as much as $16,000," and a much more speculative loss of up to $70,000. These foregone revenues are so small that they cannot provide a significant counterweight to the harm caused to AWR. In addition, as noted above, the Forest Service's opportunity to mitigate mistletoe infestation and to replant Douglas firs is tied to whether the Project occurs or not. Because we conclude that the risk that the project will not occur at all is speculative, those lost opportunities similarly cannot outweigh the harm to AWR.

The balance of the hardships here tips sharply enough in favor of AWR that a preliminary injunction is warranted in light of the serious questions raised as to the merits of its ARA claim. That decision, however, does not end our analysis, as the preliminary injunction must also be in the public interest.

4. Public Interest

In this case, we must consider competing public interests. On the side of issuing the injunction, we recognize the well-established "public interest in preserving nature and avoiding irreparable environmental injury." *Lands Council,* 537 F.3d at 1005. This court has also recognized the public interest in careful consideration of environmental impacts before major federal projects go forward, and we have held that suspending such projects until that consideration occurs "comports with the public interest." *S. Fork Band Council,* 588 F.3d at 728. While that public interest is most often noted in the context of NEPA cases, we see no reason why it does not apply equally to violations of the ARA. In the ARA, Congress specifically identified the process through which it wanted the Forest Service to make project decisions such as this one. It comports with the public interest for the Forest Service to comply faithfully with those procedures and to use the exceptional emergency procedures sparingly and only in compliance with its own implementing regulations.

We will not grant a preliminary injunction, however, unless those public interests outweigh other public interests that cut in favor of *not* issuing the injunction. (citation omitted). "The public interest analysis for the issuance of a preliminary injunction requires us to consider whether there exists some critical public interest that would be injured by the grant of preliminary relief." *Cal. Pharmacists Ass'n v. Maxwell-Jolly,* 596 F.3d 1098, 1114–15 (9th Cir. 2010) (internal quotations omitted).

The public interests that might be injured by a preliminary injunction here, however, do not outweigh the public interests that will be served. The primary public interest asserted by the Forest Service is that the Project will aid the struggling local economy and prevent job loss. The effect on the health of the local economy is a proper consideration in the public interest analysis. The Forest Service asserts that the Project would directly create 18 to 26 temporary jobs and would have indirect beneficial effects on other aspects of the local economy. The record before us reflects that the jobs in question, and, for the most part, the indirect effects, will begin and end with work on the Project which is now expected to be completed in 2010.

On these facts, we conclude that issuing the injunction is in the public interest.

C. *North Atlantic Instruments, Inc. v. Haber et al.*, 188 F.3d 38 (2d Cir. 1999)

STRAUB, Circuit Judge:

The defendants-appellants, Fred Haber and Apex Signal Corp., appeal from an order of the United States District Court for the Eastern District of New York (Arthur D. Spatt, Judge) preliminarily enjoining them from, *inter alia*, soliciting particular client contacts contained in a list allegedly misappropriated from the plaintiff-appellee, North Atlantic Instruments, Inc. (The) District Court relied in large part on findings of fact and conclusions of law presented in Report and Recommendation by the Magistrate Judge who had held an extensive, eight-day evidentiary hearing. Based on the Report and Recommendation and its own review of the record, the District Court concluded, *inter alia*, that the list of client contacts prepared and used by Haber while Haber was an employee of North Atlantic constituted a protectable trade secret and that the defendants were bound not to use the information contained in the list. In light of those findings the District Court entered a preliminary injunction against the defendants.

This appeal requires us to decide whether the District Court permissibly restricted the defendants from soliciting North Atlantic's customers through the individual client contacts that Haber had developed while at North Atlantic and its predecessor. Because we conclude that the District Court did not exceed its allowable discretion in doing so, we affirm.

BACKGROUND

On August 31, 1994, North Atlantic entered into an Asset Purchase Agreement with Transmagnetics, Inc. ("TMI"). North Atlantic designs and manufactures specialized, technical, industrial electronics equipment. At the time North Atlantic acquired TMI, Haber was a one-third owner of TMI, its president, and the head of sales—a position which allowed him to develop extensive client contacts. North Atlantic's chief executive testified that the specialized and customized nature of TMI's business made the identity of the relatively small numbers of engineers who required its products especially crucial to its business success. That is, there may be only two engineers—within a company comprised of 20,000 engineers and 100,000 employees—who might need the technology produced by TMI. As a result, he concluded, knowing the identity and needs of these engineers was an extremely valuable aspect of TMI's business and one that would have been very difficult for any company to derive on its own. In part because of this, North Atlantic evidently conditioned its purchase of TMI on Haber's continuing to work for North Atlantic in a similar role to that which he had occupied at TMI.

The Asset Purchase Agreement provided that TMI would sell and transfer to North Atlantic "all of the properties and assets of every kind, nature and description, real, personal or mixed, tangible or intangible." Specifically itemized within these assets were "all . . . customer and vendor databases" and "all goodwill and other intangible assets, owned, used or held for use by [TMI]" in its business. Consistent with this language, North Atlantic's owner testified that the list of client contacts presumably included within these intangible assets was "a very important aspect of the purchase." North Atlantic paid $99,667 for TMI's fixed assets, a portion of which included goodwill, and $851,134 for TMI's inventory. In addition, North Atlantic clearly valued the information that Haber brought to bear, as demonstrated by its paying him salary and bonuses of approximately $300,000 in his first year with North Atlantic.

Shortly after the acquisition, on November 7, 1994, North Atlantic entered into an employment agreement (the "Employment Agreement") with Haber. In it, Haber expressly agreed:

> . . . to keep secret and retain in the strictest confidence all confidential matters which relate to [North Atlantic], including, without limitation, customer lists, trade secrets, pricing policies and other confidential business affairs of [North Atlantic] . . . and any affiliate . . . and not to disclose any such confidential matter to anyone outside [North Atlantic] or any affiliate . . .

The terms of this provision apply both "during and after his period of service with [North Atlantic]," and the agreement required that Haber turn over, upon his termination, all documents and property of North Atlantic that contained any confidential information.

In July 1997, Haber left North Atlantic to join Apex Signal Corp., a company that manufactures products targeting the same niche market as North Atlantic's TMI division. North Atlantic argues that after Haber joined Apex, Apex changed its focus from more general purpose products to the customized products produced by TMI and later by North Atlantic's TMI division. . . . (As) soon as Haber left North Atlantic and began work for Apex, he began calling the client contacts he had used and developed while at North Atlantic and TMI, and asking that they leave North Atlantic to do business with Apex.

. . . North Atlantic produced a printout of confidential client information from North Atlantic's customer database, printed by Haber on September 5, 1997—over one month after he had left North Atlantic—and found in Apex's files. . . . Testimony at the hearing suggested that it would have been impossible for Haber to have generated this information unless he had taken files with him when he left North Atlantic. Finally, evidence at the hearing indicated that Haber had in other instances used his contacts and product and pricing information from his time at North Atlantic to solicit customers for Apex.

Procedural History is omitted. Complaint and Preliminary Injunction filed. Injunction granted.

Haber and Apex appear to accept much of the preliminary injunction and now appeal only the portion of the District Court's order forbidding Haber and Apex from soliciting the contacts Haber developed while at North Atlantic and TMI.

I. Applicable Standards

DISCUSSION

"A party seeking a preliminary injunction must establish that (1) absent injunctive relief, it will suffer irreparable harm, and (2) either (a) that it is likely to succeed on the merits, or (b) that there are sufficiently serious questions going to the merits to make them a fair ground for litigation, and that the balance of hardships tips decidedly in favor of the moving party."

* * *

II. Likelihood of Success on the Merits

To succeed on a claim for the misappropriation of trade secrets under New York law, a party must demonstrate: (1) that it possessed a trade secret, and (2) that the defendants used that trade secret in breach of an agreement, confidential relationship or duty, or as a result of discovery by improper means. . . .

A. North Atlantic's Client Contacts as Trade Secrets

We first consider whether the District Court properly concluded that North Atlantic's client list, which contains the identities and preferences of its client contacts, constitutes a protectable trade secret. As explained below, we hold that the District Court did not exceed its allowable discretion in determining that it does.

"[A] trade secret is any formula, pattern, device or compilation of information which is used in one's business, and which gives [the owner] an opportunity to obtain an advantage over competitors who do not know or use it." (citations omitted). In determining whether information constitutes a trade secret, New York courts have considered the following factors:

> (1) the extent to which the information is known outside of the business;
> (2) the extent to which it is known by employees and others involved in the business; (3) the extent of measures taken by the business to guard the secrecy of the information; (4) the value of the information to the business and its competitors; (5) the amount of effort or money expended by the business in developing the information; (6) the ease or difficulty with which the information could be properly acquired or duplicated by others.

* * *

As explained below, the Magistrate Judge's factual determination—which the District Court adopted—exhaustively considered the relevant factors as laid out by the Restatement and concluded that the list of client contacts was a protectable trade secret. This finding was not clearly erroneous.

The Magistrate Judge concluded that the list of *companies* to whom North Atlantic's TMI division sold was not a trade secret. In this respect, the Magistrate Judge found that North Atlantic had not proven that such a list "could not have been developed by reviewing, among other public sources, trade publications available to anyone who availed himself or herself [of] such reference." He further noted that "importantly, the TMI catalog [, which is a public document,] contained a list of its primary customers and the military projects in which TMI products were used." By contrast, the Magistrate Judge determined that the *identities of individual contact people* with whom Haber dealt while at North Atlantic or TMI were protectable trade secrets.

The Magistrate Judge began his analysis for this second conclusion by determining that information on specific contact people was "not readily available" to others in the industry. That is, Haber generated the list of specific contact people—the people who required the customized technology produced by TMI and North Atlantic's TMI division—over the fifty years he had worked in the industry, more than half of which he spent at TMI. The Magistrate Judge relied in his finding on the testimony of North Atlantic's chief executive, who described the needle-in-the-haystack character of the search for the handful of engineers in companies of 100,000 employees who might have a use for one of North Atlantic's customized products.

The Magistrate Judge went on to consider the third Restatement factor, concluding that North Atlantic took numerous appropriate measures to prevent unauthorized disclosure of the information contained in its list of client contacts. In his analysis, the Magistrate Judge looked to several confidentiality agreements signed or agreed to by Haber and other North Atlantic employees. Most pertinently, the Employment Agreement itself contains an express non-disclosure provision requiring that Haber "keep secret and retain in the strictest confidence all confidential matters which relate to [North Atlantic], including, without limitation, customer lists [and] trade secrets." Second, the Magistrate Judge noted that all North Atlantic employees, including Haber, signed a more general confidentiality provision in an Employee's Handbook. Third, the Magistrate Judge pointed to a separate employee confidentiality agreement that recognizes that an employee's services at North Atlantic will "expose [the employee] to . . . information or data with respect to . . . lists of actual and prospective customers." Accordingly, the employee "agrees to keep secret all such confidential matters [and] . . . further acknowledges and agrees that all such information and materials constitute trade secrets of [North Atlantic]." Fourth, a similar confidentiality agreement existed during Haber's years as president of TMI requiring that employees not "divulge . . . any information which has come into [their] possession as a result of [their] employment with [TMI] to any third parties, *including . . . customer lists.*" (emphasis added). Finally, the Magistrate Judge noted that North Atlantic's "computers require each user to input a password in order to gain access to the system and, upon entry, a [confidentiality] warning message is displayed." Indeed, access to the database containing the list of client contacts was restricted to only seven or eight employees out of seventy on a "need to know" basis. In light of this analysis, the Magistrate Judge concluded that North Atlantic had taken sufficient measures to safeguard the confidentiality of its client contact list.

The Magistrate Judge next assessed the value of the list of client contacts and the energy and effort necessary to create it. In this respect, he pointed to testimony by North Atlantic's chief executive stating that "in the technology business, the most expensive thing to replicate is your relationship with your customers. That's the value of a company, the collective relationships and goodwill and reputation that you have garnered in the industry." Additionally, the Magistrate Judge noted that North Atlantic had paid for TMI's assets, including intangible goodwill.

The Magistrate Judge's findings with regard to the time and effort required to create the list of client contacts, as well as the lack of the general availability of such customer information to others in the trade, are amply supported in the record. Likewise, the record buttresses the Magistrate Judge's determination that North Atlantic made clear the importance of maintaining the confidentiality of the client contact list both to its employees generally and to Haber in particular. In light of the care with which North Atlantic guarded this information and the plain terms of the Employment Agreement, it would be difficult to conclude that Haber was unable to discern his responsibilities with respect to his client contact list. Particularly given the deference due a district court in determining the appropriateness of a preliminary injunction, we cannot hold that, in this case, the adoption of the Magistrate Judge's Report and Recommendation on this point was clearly erroneous.

III. Irreparable Harm

* * *

Finally, we conclude that North Atlantic has shown that it will suffer irreparable harm in the absence of an injunction. We have held that "loss of trade secrets cannot be measured in money damages" because "[a] trade secret once lost is, of course, lost forever." *FMC Corp. v. Taiwan Tainan Giant Indus. Co.*, 730 F.2d 61, 63 (2d Cir. 1984) (per curiam). In addition, Haber acknowledged in his Employment Agreement that a breach of the confidentiality clause would cause "irreparable injury" to North Atlantic. In light of our holding in FMC and the "irreparable injury" clause in the Employment Agreement, we conclude that North Atlantic would be irreparably harmed in the absence of an injunction.

CONCLUSION

Because North Atlantic has demonstrated a likelihood of success on the merits and because it would suffer irreparable harm in the absence of an injunction, we conclude that the District Court did not exceed its allowable discretion in granting a preliminary injunction. We therefore affirm.

VAN GRAAFEILAND, Circuit Judge, dissenting:

Perhaps the best approach in deciding the legality of an order is to determine exactly what the order says. This is particularly true where disobedience of the order is punishable as a contempt of court. Every order granting an injunction must be specific in its terms, Fed. R. Civ. P. 65(d). The party enjoined "must be able to ascertain from the four corners of the order precisely what acts are forbidden." *Sanders v. Air Line Pilots Ass'n., Int'l.*, 473 F.2d 244, 247 (2d Cir. 1972). "Basic fairness requires that those enjoined receive explicit notice of precisely what conduct is outlawed." *Schmidt v. Lessard*, 414 U.S. 473, 476, 38 L. Ed. 2d 661, 94 S. Ct. 713 (1974). "The judicial contempt power is a potent weapon. When it is founded upon a decree too vague to be understood, it can be a deadly one." *International Longshoremen's Ass'n. Local 1291 v. Philadelphia Marine Trade Ass'n.*, 389 U.S. 64, 76, 19 L. Ed. 2d 236, 88 S. Ct. 201 (1967). . . .

When I examine the order in the instant case with the foregoing admonitions in mind, I am troubled with the very first sentence which enjoins the defendants "from using any of plaintiff's trade secrets or proprietary information." There is no clear and readily understandable definition of the term "trade secret." *See Ashland Management, Inc. v. Janien*, 82 N.Y.2d 395, 407, 604 N.Y.S.2d 912, 624 N.E.2d 1007 (1993). In determining whether a trade secret exists, . . . A defendant enjoined from using a "trade secret" . . . does not know precisely what he is forbidden from doing. To avoid contempt, he has to follow the same process as do the courts, with no assurance of reaching the same result. It follows that when as here there is any ambiguity about what constitutes a trade secret, we should not affirm an injunction order that forbids its "use." Indeed, the word "use" itself is troublesome. Ordinarily, a trade secret is violated by its disclosure, not its use. The two words are not synonymous. One may use information without disclosing it. This brings us to the term "customer contact" as used in the injunction order. . . . The only way in which Haber and Apex could be assured of avoiding all of these "contacts" would be to go out of business—to discontinue building a "better mousetrap" than was being built by plaintiff. . . .

D. *American Red Cross v. Palm Beach Blood Bank, Inc.*, 143 F.3d 1407 (11th Cir. 1998)

BIRCH, Circuit Judge:

In this diversity case, we review the propriety of a preliminary injunction entered against one blood bank to prohibit it from using "trade secret" donor lists compiled by another, competing blood bank. On appeal from the district court's injunction, [Palm Beach] argues both that [the] lists are not protectable trade secrets and that the injunction is impermissibly vague. We vacate the injunction and remand the case to the district court for further proceedings.

I. BACKGROUND

Defendant-appellant, Palm Beach Blood Bank, Inc. ("Palm Beach"), is a nonprofit Florida corporation engaged in the business of collecting, processing, and distributing blood components. Similarly, plaintiff-appellee, American Red Cross ("Red Cross"), is also a nonprofit corporation engaged in collecting, processing, and distributing blood components, though its activities are more national in scope. . . . Palm Beach and Red Cross compete with each other for sponsors and donors. Competition between the two companies is especially keen regarding recruitment of apheresis donors, a small subset of blood donors willing to undergo a longer and less-comfortable donation procedure.

Palm Beach opened a Miami branch and over the next several months hired a number of Red Cross's Miami personnel. At least one of these former Red Cross employees took a list of Red Cross donors with her to Palm Beach, where she used the list to contact and recruit blood donors for her new employer. Soon after opening its Miami office, Palm Beach succeeded in recruiting several former Red Cross donors, including apheresis donors, to participate in Palm Beach's blood collection program.

Red Cross discovered that Palm Beach was using at least one of Red Cross's donor lists for Palm Beach's own solicitations

The Procedural history is omitted. A complaint, TRO and PI were filed and granted.

(T)he district court entered the following preliminary injunction that restrained Palm Beach from:

> (a) possessing, copying, or making unauthorized use of Plaintiff's lists or any other documents that contain trade secrets that are the proprietary property of Plaintiff;

> (b) contacting and/or soliciting donations from any donor whose name is contained on Plaintiff's lists;

> (c) engaging in any other activity constituting a misappropriation of Plaintiff's lists, or in any way adversely affecting Plaintiff's reputation or goodwill;

> (d) using any false designation of origin or false description which can or is likely to lead the trade or public or individual members thereof to erroneously believe that Defendant is affiliated with Plaintiff;

> (e) disposing of or destroying any documents that are relevant to the Complaint in this action, including but not limited to Plaintiff's lists, or Defendant's donor lists, or donor information, whether in hard copy form or on a computer, or any simulation or copy thereof, or any document or computer data which has its genesis from any of Plaintiff's lists;

> (f) disposing of or destroying any documents or related materials that evidence, relate, or pertain to Defendant's misappropriation of Plaintiff's lists, as well as the records of donations solicited and obtained from Plaintiff's donors.

Soon thereafter, Palm Beach filed an emergency motion for clarification, expressing concern that the injunction appeared to allow Red Cross to determine which of Palm Beach's competitive practices were illegitimate (and which therefore might lead to sanctions for contempt). . . .

II. DISCUSSION

The discussion of whether these lists were trade secrets is omitted. The court found that the names of the customers that had been published in catalogues and trade publications were no longer secrets, but that other, more detailed informations were entitled to trade secret protection.

B. THE SCOPE OF THE PRELIMINARY INJUNCTION

Palm Beach argues that several provisions of the preliminary injunction are so vague as to violate Rule 65(d) of the Federal Rules of Civil Procedure ("Rule 65(d)"). As we have previously held, a court must craft its orders so that those who seek to obey may know precisely what the court intends to forbid. . . . Thus, Rule 65(d) of the Federal Rules of Civil Procedure provides that "every order granting an injunction . . . shall be specific in terms; [and] shall describe in reasonable detail . . . the act or acts sought to be restrained. . . ." Fed.R.Civ.P. 65(d). Under this rule, "an ordinary person reading the court's order should be able to ascertain from the document itself exactly what conduct is proscribed. *American Red Cross*, 143 F.3d at 1411 (citations omitted).

Applying Rule 65(d), we believe that two significant portions of the injunction do not give Palm Beach sufficient notice as to what actions the district court means to prohibit. First, the injunction prohibits "contacting and/or soliciting donations from any donor whose name is contained on Plaintiff's lists." Although at first glance this directive from the district court may seem simple enough, Palm Beach has no way to determine whether a given member of the public might happen to appear on a Red Cross list not in Palm Beach's possession. . . .

Since an ordinary person in Palm Beach's position could not ascertain which members of the public might be off-limits for its recruitment efforts, this provision contravenes Rule 65(d).

Second, the injunction bars Palm Beach from "possessing, copying, or making unauthorized use of Plaintiff's lists or any other documents that contain trade secrets that are the proprietary property of Plaintiff." R2-46-2. (emphasis added). As Red Cross argues, a nonspecific injunction may sometimes be justified "when the information needed to make the order specific in form is known only to the party to be enjoined." . . . In this case, though, Red Cross has not suggested even a genre of trade secret beyond its donor lists that Palm Beach might misappropriate, nor has Red Cross explained why only Palm Beach should be thought to have knowledge of those Red Cross trade secrets that the injunction might protect. Indeed, the lack of any apparent factual basis for this open-ended portion of the injunction has left Palm Beach understandably uncertain as to what the district court means to prohibit. While we would not expect an injunction in a case such as the one at bar to describe with particularity each of the documents that Palm Beach might misappropriate, we do think that the district court's injunction should put Palm Beach on notice as to the types of information, "other" than "lists," to which it applies. ....The district court may not simply order Palm Beach to "obey the law." . . .

Finally, we note that, assuming Red Cross's lists are protectable trade secrets, the district court could readily have drafted a narrower injunction. Such an injunction would presumably have prohibited Palm

Beach from (1) possessing, using, or copying Red Cross's lists or any other specific types of valuable confidential documents identified by the district court, (2) using false designations or descriptions to mislead individuals or businesses into believing that Palm Beach is affiliated with Red Cross, and (3) disposing of or destroying material evidence. Such an injunction would have given Palm Beach much fairer notice of what the district court intended to prohibit, without compromising whatever legitimate need Red Cross may have for protection of its trade secrets.

In sum, the district court has crafted an injunction that leaves Palm Beach without reasonable notice of what the court means to prohibit. Regardless of whatever assurances Red Cross may have given the district court or Palm Beach regarding its intended manner of enforcing the injunction, Palm Beach should not have to risk citation for contempt in order to determine the true scope of activity barred by the district court's order. . . . Therefore, we hold that the preliminary injunction is impermissibly vague under Rule 65(d), and we vacate the district court's order.

III. CONCLUSION

In its attempt to protect Red Cross from misappropriation of its trade secrets, the district court has fashioned an injunction that is impermissibly vague under Rule 65(d). . . . Therefore, we VACATE the preliminary injunction and REMAND this case to the district court for further development of the record and entry of more particularized findings of fact. If, upon reconsideration, the district court concludes that Red Cross can show a substantial likelihood of success on the merits of its claims, the district court may craft a more narrow injunction to protect Red Cross's rights from abuse by Palm Beach.